THE LIVI ✌ P9-BJQ-932

The Greatest
Old Testament Words

EDGAR JONES

*Professor of Hebrew and Old Testament
in the Northern Congregational College,
Manchester*

With a Preface by
Professor William Barclay

SCM PRESS LTD
BLOOMSBURY STREET LONDON

For

E.J., V.J., and G.J.

FIRST PUBLISHED 1964
© SCM PRESS LTD 1964
PRINTED IN GREAT BRITAIN BY
CHARLES BIRCHALL & SONS LTD
LIVERPOOL AND LONDON

NOTE

THE present study arose from an attempt to share the riches of the Hebrew Bible with students at the Northern Congregational College. The transliteration of the Hebrew words is as found in Robert Young's *Analytical Concordance to the Bible* (eighth edition, 1939), with the addition of *alephs* (') and *ayins* ('). This will be found to vary at points from later scholars but has been used because this concordance is far and away the best tool for the preacher. I have selected some of the key words and commented on them only in some contexts. Should the reader examine these words further and use the same method to look at other words he cannot fail to reap a rich harvest for himself and his congregation.

I am greatly indebted to the Rev. William Hodgkins, then Editor of the *Congregational Monthly*, who invited me to contribute some of these studies to that journal and consented to my using the material in another form in this volume. My warmest appreciation is offered to the Rev. David L. Edwards, Editor of the SCM Press, for his encouragement, and to the readers of the Press for their comments; to Mrs D. Wallwork for typing the original draft; and to the Rev. Roger Tomes for his kindness in commenting on the MS.

Dr William Barclay has honoured me in contributing his Preface to Preachers and I am deeply grateful to him.

EDGAR JONES

CONTENTS

III · CONCERNING THE COMMUNITY AND THE CULT

A PREFACE TO PREACHERS

MOST people are intensely interested in facts, especially if these facts are attractively presented. Most people are eager and willing to listen to new and interesting information. Unless a man is really famous, few people are interested in listening to his opinion about the latest political crisis, the most recent television play, the newest literary scandal.

If this is true—and it is true—then a man has the best chance of being listened to when he talks about that on which he has some claims to be an expert. People will listen to him, if they believe that he has some qualifications which give him the right to speak.

When we apply these general rules to the particular work of the preacher, then one thing stands out—*the Church needs to set the teaching ministry in the very forefront of its activities. The* public knows quite well that the parson is no political expert and no literary or dramatic critic; the public is not particularly interested in hearing him fulminate as a censor of morals. But the public does rightly or wrongly believe that this man has had a theological education. They know that he has studied in a theological college or in the Divinity Faculty of a University in which he may even have acquired a theological degree. They are therefore prepared to listen to him when he preaches on the things about which it may be assumed that he knows something, while at best they may tolerate him, and at worst they may laugh at him, and practically always they will disregard him, when he holds forth on subjects on which he is but ill qualified to pronounce.

The parson then ought to be a teacher of that which he knows. What then shall he teach?

The Church in all its branches has never been in any doubt that it regards the Bible as the supreme rule of faith and life. That belief is in fact written into the fundamental statements of most Churches. Now if the Bible is the supreme rule of faith and life, the essential of all essentials is to know what it is saying, and to know as accurately as possible. It is further necessary to approach the Bible in such a way that the preacher is expounding its truth and not reading his particular beliefs and even prejudices into it, or extracting them from it.

The conclusion is clear and inescapable—*the study of the Bible must begin with the study of words*. Whether we like it or not, theology must begin from lexicography. Only there can speculation be anchored in belief, and only then can the structure of theology be raised upon the foundation of biblical revelation.

Words then are the raw material of all theology, and, therefore, anyone who helps us to define the meaning of the great biblical words is rendering a real service to the preacher and to the Church. This is what Dr Edgar Jones has done for the great words of the Old Testament.

The task of him who would do this for the Old Testament is at once much easier and much more difficult than the task of him who would do it for the New Testament. It is easier because the vocabulary of Hebrew is much smaller than the vocabulary of Greek, and the Hebrew words do not have the infinite shades of meaning which can attach to a Greek word. The area of research is therefore much more limited. On the other hand, it is more difficult because the New Testament word student has the whole of Greek literature from which he may illustrate and define the meaning of his words, whereas the Old Testament word student has to all intents and purposes nothing outside the Old Testament to which he can go for light on his words.

Dr Jones has done his task well. Here are discussions of such great words as covenant, kingdom, law, holiness, sin, atonement,

Satan, Messiah, redeemer. And it is to be noted that this book is not an essay in lexicography; it is an experiment in communication. This *is* the material of preaching. No one can read this book without acquiring a fund of knowledge which is bound to enrich his preaching and a sharpness of definition which is bound to make his preaching more effective.

One of the great dangers of religious speaking and writing is that words begin to be used conventionally, and their real meaning is forgotten. And, as one great preacher put it: 'The worn coin will not operate the slot machine.' Words need to be rediscovered, redefined, reminted. This is precisely what Dr Jones does. If the preacher reads and studies and uses this book, words which were fossilized will spring to life again; words which were dull and inert will be seen to be dynamic, explosive units of energy, clamouring to be preached about.

The preacher does not need to know Hebrew to use this book. All the words are transliterated into English; but this book will enable even the non-linguist to speak with authority about the words of the Old Testament. Through it the teaching of the Old Testament will come alive and will be seen to be still astonishingly relevant after all the centuries even for today.

Trinity College,
Glasgow

WILLIAM BARCLAY

INTRODUCTION

Why the Old Testament?

FOR a large part of the Christian Church the Old Testament is either a lost book or at best a neglected one. Because of a false antithesis the God of the Old Testament is thought of as the Lawgiver and Judge whilst the God of the New Testament is associated with Love and Grace. To correct this travesty of the truth we must examine more closely the relationship between the Old Testament and the Christian Faith. In what sense can we say that the Old Testament contains the Word of God for our day?

We may remind ourselves of three basic principles:

The Old Testament was the Scripture used by Jesus and the disciples. It is to the Old Testament that Jesus turned to find a way of expressing his self-chosen role to give his life a ransom for many.[1] It is the Old Testament that contains the self-designation the Son of Man[2] and in the words of the Deuteronomic writer Jesus meets the challenge of the Temptations in the wilderness as he considers the way in which he would carry out his mission.[3] The Old Testament is the glorious heritage of Jesus and we cannot hope to understand his words or actions without considering the creative influences of his own background.

The New Testament presupposes the teaching of the Old Testament. Without the teaching of the Old Testament the record of the New Testament at some points would be incomplete as an

[1] See Mark 10.45 and Isa. 53.12.
[2] See Dan. 7.13.
[3] See Deut. 6.13, 16; 8.3; Ps. 91.11–12.

account of Christian belief. Thus, the Fatherhood of God does not emerge suddenly in the New Testament but is already central in many Old Testament writings.[1]

Especially in the field of Christian ethical thought and social teaching is the Old Testament presupposed. The social teaching of the prophets forms the source from which the teaching of the Sermon on the Mount and the Pauline ethical teaching in the Letter to the Romans derive their inspiration.

The Old Testament and the New Testament are integrally connected. A recent comment has been made that aptly describes the underlying unity of the two testaments. 'Speaking figuratively, we may say that the events of the Old Testament are like the first two acts of a play, incomplete in themselves without the final act. We should also say that though the events of the New Testament contain the crisis and denouement of the final act, they cannot be fully understood without the first two acts. The Early Church understood the Old Testament in this light. We should never forget that the Old Testament was the Holy Scripture of the Early Church—the only Scripture it had at first. It was the Bible of Jesus and Paul.'[2]

Interpreting the Old Testament

The Old Testament may be approached in a number of ways that have long left behind the attempt to ransack it for proof texts to bolster up a system of ideas already reached. Rather we would suggest that 'in order to understand the Old Testament we have to listen to the New, and that in order to be able to interpret the New Testament we have to know the Old'.[3]

In recent research four basic approaches have been made to the Old Testament and its interpretation.

[1] See Hos. 11.1–4; Jer. 3.19.
[2] See Dwight E. Stevenson, *Preaching on the Books of the Old Testament*, New York, Harper, 1961, p. 6.
[3] See the volume edited by Claus Westermann, *Essays on Old Testament Interpretation*, London, SCM Press, 1964, p. 12.

i. *The Old Testament and Typology.* The heart of this method of approaching the Old Testament has been to regard the events of the Old Testament as not of primary significance for themselves but as foreshadowing the events of the Gospel and the New Testament. The unreality of such interpretations is seen when we find such a typological method used in the exegesis of the early Fathers and Isaac is seen as a type of Christ and since the meaning of his name is 'Laughter' this represents the joy of the faithful which is given by Christ,[1] or the correspondence that is supposed to exist between the scarlet cord of Rahab and the blood of Christ.[2] The real issue is however not whether any typology can ever be justified but can we distinguish between legitimate and fanciful typology? In contrast to the excesses of the examples given above we may see a positive value in linking the role of the Suffering Servant of Deutero-Isaiah and the mission of Christ—a relation that Christ himself acknowledges So in the Letter to the Hebrews we are greatly helped by realizing the correspondence between the description of the work and person of Christ given there and the role of the High Priest in the rites of the Day of Atonement.

The safeguard must always be that we take the historical character of the Old Testament seriously. This will save us from the dangers of allegorism which carried to its logical conclusion would mean that we could dispense with the Scripture itself.[3] The persons and events of the Old Testament may not be approached as shadows in an unsubstantial world, just pawns or counters in some master plan. Remembering this historical framework of God's revelation we may 'really speak of a witness of the Old Testament to Christ, for our knowledge of Christ is incomplete without the witness of the Old Testament. Christ is given to us only through the double witness of the choir of those who await and those who remember. . . . But the Old Testament must

[1] See G. W. H. Lampe and K. J. Woollcombe, *Essays on Typology*, London, SCM Press, 1957, p. 32.
[2] *Op. cit.*, p. 33.
[3] *Ibid.*

first of all be heard in its witness to the creative Word of God in history; and in these dealings of God in history, in his acts of judgment as well as in his acts of redemption, we may everywhere discern what is already a Christ-event.'[1]

ii. *The Old Testament and the Confession of Faith.* By this approach we break away from seeing in the Old Testament just a history of the Hebrew people with an account of their religious ideas and institutions. The theology of the Old Testament is more than the sum total of separate concepts. Rather we may see in the Old Testament, 'the confessional recital of the redemptive acts of God in a particular history, because history is the medium of revelation'.[2] The same writer, G. E. Wright, continues in defining the sense in which history is to be understood in approaching the Old Testament: 'It is history as the arena of God's activity. Biblical theology is first and foremost a theology of recital, in which biblical man confesses his faith by reciting the formative events of his history as the redemptive handiwork of God. The realism of the Bible consists in its close attention to the facts of history and tradition because these are the facts of God.'[3]

Two examples will illustrate the value of this approach to the interpretation of the Old Testament. The first confession is used at the central sanctuary when first fruits are being brought to the tabernacle:

> An Aramean ready to perish was my father; and he went down into Egypt and sojourned there with a few, and became there a nation ... And the Egyptians ... laid upon us hard bondage ... And the Lord brought us forth out of Egypt with a mighty hand ... And he hath brought us into this place, and hath given us this land (Deut. 2.5-9).[4]

[1] See the essay by Gerhard von Rad, 'The Typological Interpretation of the Old Testament' in the volume, Claus Westermann (ed.), *Essays on Old Testament Interpretation*, p. 39.
[2] G. E. Wright, *God Who Acts*, London, SCM Press, 1952, p. 13.
[3] *Op. cit.*, p. 38.
[4] The translation follows that of Wright, *op. cit.*, p. 71.

Here we have a *credo* which recites the acts of God that brought into being the people of God. Again in Deuteronomy 6 we read:

> And when your son asks you in time to come, 'What is the mean-- ing of the testimonies and the statutes and the ordinances which the Lord our God has commanded you?' then you shall say to your son, 'We were Pharaoh's slaves in Egypt; and the Lord brought us out of Egypt with a mighty hand; and the Lord showed us signs and wonders, great and grievous ... and he brought *us* out from there that he might bring us in and give *us* the land which he swore to give to our fathers' (vv. 20-23).

The significance of these passages may be seen in the elements of a confession of faith that they contain. First, God's election of Abraham, secondly, his deliverance of his people at the Exodus and followed by his gift of the Promised land.[1] The Old Testament contains a *kerygma* as surely as the New Testament.[2]

iii. *The Old Testament and Re-Presentation.* A further approach to the interpretation of the Old Testament is found in the recognition that the writers offer a re-presentation of historical events. Two examples will illuminate this characteristic. The Festival of the Passover and Unleavened Bread is a combination of a nomadic sacrificial rite designed to ward off danger from the herds and flocks, and an agricultural festival held in order to dedicate the grain at the beginning of the harvest. However, in Israel the festival is specifically linked with the Exodus, that is, a re-creation of the situation as the Israelites set out from Egypt. So we read:

> Observe the month of Abib, and keep the passover to the Lord your God; for in the month of Abib the Lord your God brought you out of Egypt by night. And you shall offer the passover sacrifice to the Lord your God, from the flock of the herd, at the place which the Lord will choose, to make his name dwell there. You shall eat no leavened bread with it; seven days you shall

---

[1] See also Josh. 24.2–13; Ps. 77.12; Ps. 78; Ps. 105; Ps. 136.
[2] See Acts 3.22-23 and Wright, *op. cit.*, pp. 62, 68.

eat it with unleavened bread, the bread of affliction—for you came out of the land of Egypt in hurried flight—that all the days of your life you may remember the day when you came out of the land of Egypt.[1]

A further example is found in the account of the Feast of Tabernacles where the custom of living in 'booths' for the purpose of harvesting fruit is directly linked with the period of the Israelite wilderness wanderings and deliberately re-created for each generation. So we read in Leviticus:

You shall dwell in booths for seven days; all that are native in Israel shall dwell in booths, that your generations may know that I made the people of Israel dwell in booths when I brought them out of the land of Egypt: I am the Lord God.[2]

Of great importance is the reference found in Deut. 5.3 where the Decalogue is proclaimed:

The Lord our God made a covenant with *us* in Horeb. Not with our fathers did the Lord make this covenant, but with *us*, who are all of *us* here alive *this day*.

The hearers are conscious that they themselves are standing to receive the commands of God as if the situation at Mount Horeb is re-presented to them. The characteristic of 're-presentation' is further evident in the frequently recurring use of the word 'today' in Deuteronomy.[3]

This 're-presentation' may also refer to the future; events are spoken of as if they had already taken place. In the Psalms we find that the cry 'Yahweh is king' is pronounced as if he was being enthroned at that very moment and in for example Psalm 47 the reference is to the future reign of God as already consummated:

God reigns over the nations;
God sits on his holy throne.

[1] See Deut. 16.1–3 and Ex. 12.11.
[2] Lev. 23.42–43 and see also Ex. 12.24; Deut. 31.10–13.
[3] See Deut. 26.16–19.

The princes of the peoples gather as the peoples of the God of
Abraham
For the shields of the earth belong to God;
he is highly exalted (vv. 8-10).

The manner of this re-presenting is by the proclamation of the
saving acts of God, by the telling forth. In Ex. 12.24-27a, we read
concerning the Passover rites:

And when your children say to you, 'What do you mean by this
service?' you shall say, 'It is the sacrifice of the Lord's passover,
for he passed over the houses of the people of Israel in Egypt,
when he slew the Egyptians but spared our houses.'

The underlying conviction is 'that God and his action are always
present, while man in his inevitable temporality cannot grasp
this present-ness except by "re-presenting" the acts of God over
and over again in his worship.'[1] It is this spirit and attitude that
characterizes our own approach to the Birth, Crucifixion and
Resurrection of Christ for without their *present-ness* we remain
outside and the Bible record is just a museum piece of antiquity.

Karl Barth has expressed the heart of the matter in these words:
'In revelation we deal with a "news report", or better said, with
"a sheaf of news reports", and these "news reports written in
words" appear in a "book of the Old and New Testaments";
and we have to ask what these "news reports" say, and we have
to pass them on just as they are.'[2]

iv. *Promise and Fulfilment in the Old Testament.* A fourth
insight into the nature of the Old Testament records is
afforded by the theme of Promise and Fulfilment. A recent
estimate has been that 'When we survey the entire Old Testament
we find ourselves involved in a great history of movement from
promise to fulfilment. It flows like a large brook here rushing
swiftly, there apparently coming to rest in a quiet backwater and
yet moving forward as a whole toward a distant goal which lies

[1] See Claus Westermann, *op. cit.*, pp. 76–88.
[2] K. Barth cited by M. Noth in *Essays on O. T. Interpretation*, p. 88.

beyond itself.'[1] Throughout the Pentateuch, the prophetical books and the Psalter there is this expectation, the pressing forward to a new era. A characteristic phrase is 'the days are coming when'.[2] So Muilenburg writes of Israel's future, 'The time appointed her by the grace of God never permits her the security of the present. No present is ever the consummation intended or desired by God. Every present is stamped with the seal of the "not yet" ... the future is therefore the centre of gravity of Israel's faith; the mainspring of her existence; the source of her vitality, optimism and hope, the time of the resolution of all the ambiguities and inequalities of the past (Isa. 40.9-10), the dawn of a new time.'[3]

It is this idea of fulfilment and promise that best helps us to understand the relation between Old and New Testaments. There are partial fulfilments for the Israelites in such experiences as the Exodus and the Return from Exile but each fulfilment raises the question of the ultimate will of God. The New Testament stands over against these partial fulfilments and affirms the New Covenant with the New Israel and all those who stand without.

The Old Testament and Preaching

On the foundation of the various approaches outlined we may have no doubt that in preaching from the Old Testament we may proclaim the Word of God as part of God's revelation of himself and his purpose. We may suggest the following practical methods of handling the material of the Old Testament as we prepare for the pulpit.

i. *The Recurring Motif or Theme.* A fruitful task for the preacher is to trace with a concordance the way in which a single idea is used again and again in a variety of contexts. Thus we

[1] W. Zimmerli, essay 'Promise and Fulfillment' in *Essays on Old Testament Interpretation*, pp. 89–122.
[2] See Isa. 8.16; Jer. 31.31–34; Isa. 32.15–17.
[3] James Muilenburg, *The Way of Israel*, New York, Harper, 1961, pp. 128–9.

find repeatedly the idea of the Exodus—a going forth. It is implicit in the going forth of Abraham, the deliverance from Egypt and the Return from Exile. These are all variations on a theme that dominates a good deal of scripture. Again in the Book of Deuteronomy we find a repeated emphasis on the word 'today' with the underlying message of the here-and-now-ness of the demands of God to every generation.

ii. *The Search for Bible Scenes.* Another rewarding search is to look for the same scene in biblical narrative as, for example, the context of the *Court-room Trial.* This dominates the Book of Job and is frequent in Deutero-Isaiah and the other prophets.[1] We find that it is this scene that is behind the New Testament teaching concerning justification when God treats the guilty as though innocent and 'justifies' him freely. Again the *Wilderness* is a backcloth against which many significant episodes of scripture take place. The wilderness is linked with the deliverance from Egypt, the experience that sears Hebrew imagination.[2] The wilderness is the setting for Elijah and John the Baptist and in the wilderness Jesus meets the challenge of the Temptations.[3]

iii. *The Tracing of Key Ideas.* Behind these key ideas we do not mean that we put the emphasis on a series of propositions but upon the cluster of convictions and experiences that are crystallized in the use of a key word or idea. Thus the word Covenant runs throughout both Testaments. From the story of Noah to Abraham, from Jeremiah and Deutero-Isaiah to the Upper Room.[4] From such passages we could affirm that God initiates the Covenant, it describes the relation between the strong and the weak, it is corporate not individual, it must involve mission and becomes an inner personal relationship.

[1] See Job 31.35; Isa. 41. 1; 43.8; Micah 6.1.
[2] Ex. 20.2.
[3] See I Kings 17.3; Mark 1.4; Luke 4.2.
[4] See Gen. 9.8; 17.3; Jer. 31.33; Isa. 42.6; Mark 14.24.

iv. *Preaching on Old Testament Personalities.* One of the great sources of the Old Testament for preaching purposes is the wealth of its personalities.[1] We may worthily expound the message of the Old Testament through the medium of the lives and characters that people its pages. Such as Abraham the Pioneer who seeks an Abiding City; Moses the Friend of God who meets him Face to Face; Job the Triumphant Rebel rather than the Patience of Job; Hosea who finds God more fully through the break-up of his own marriage. If we take the trouble to soak ourselves in all that the Old Testament says of these and scores of other persons we may faithfully bear testimony to the unfolding purpose of God.

v. *Preaching on Old Testament Books as a Whole.* A final way of handling the Old Testament is to take the broad sweep of a complete book and expound its main burden and purpose. This will mean a selection of the central passages and the painting of a large canvas with all the exhilaration that this can give to many a congregation as we help them 'to see it whole'. Such Old Testament books as Jonah, Ruth, Amos or Ecclesiastes will lend themselves to this treatment but even the larger books too before we return to preach from a text or a passage. The books referred to would provide worthwhile expositions of such themes as The Wideness of God's Mercy, Love's Breaking of Barriers, A Straight God in a Bent World, Life's Supreme Good.

These suggestions are offered in addition to preaching on a single verse or a passage that has stimulated us in our reading. Together we thus may handle the Old Testament with a variety of approaches yet still breaking the bread of life.

The Use of Word Studies

The purpose of bringing together in the present volume this series of word studies is far removed from a desire to collect a

---

[1] See especially Fleming James, *Personalities of the Old Testament* (Scribner, 1939), now London, SCM Press.

number of unrelated observations having a lexical emphasis. It is rather, through an examination of the text of the Old Testament itself, to see how the vocabulary of the writings reveals how the great realities of God, Man and the World were thought about and so to underline the abiding insights that these words afford for every generation.

There are two main approaches that one may use in dealing with the evidence.

First, the major stress may be laid upon the etymology of the words considered. This would mean dealing with such questions as the original meaning of a word if known and the existence of similar words in the cognate languages. Although there is some value in thus knowing a word's past history, the relevant question which must be asked is—What does the word mean at this period and in this precise context?[1]

Secondly, the other approach, which these studies seek to embody, is to place the emphasis upon the use that is made of a word in the actual passage and context under consideration. Here we must note the developing and changing usage not to augment our knowledge of the words but to discover, at least in part, what imagery, symbolism and experience of life lies behind them. Thus they may prove keys to the richer understanding of the Living Word.[2]

[1] See J. Barr, *The Semantics of Biblical Language*, O.U.P., 1961, pp. 107–8, 158.

[2] See J. N. Schofield, *Introducing Old Testament Theology*, London, SCM Press, 1964, pp. 12–13.

I

CONCERNING GOD

OUR first series of words are those primarily concerning God. This division is not intended to be a watertight compartment, rigidly shut off, since this would be impossible. We cannot deal with God in the Old Testament as if he were divorced from Man or the World he has himself created. The underlying purpose is to affirm that without God's initiative, his will to reveal his purpose and nature, no theology would be possible. The following selection of words refer to aspects and attributes of God that may be seen as variations upon one theme—God Acts! As a consequence of his self-disclosure of what he has done, men have come to believe that God is and to bear witness to what he is like.

1 · **The Name of the Lord**—*shem Yahweh*

One of the fundamental characteristics of Hebrew thought is the significance attached to a person's name. The name is looked upon as a kind of description of the owner's personality. A man's name and his nature are indissolubly linked.

Name and nature. Three examples of this integral connection between name and nature may be given. In the clash between Nabal (meaning 'fool') and David the outlaw we see the folly of Nabal in not coming to terms with David by offering him food and drink (I Sam. 25). The story of Ruth contains the episode of Naomi's return to Bethlehem with its contrast to her earlier going forth. In her sorrow she cries, Call me not Naomi (happy, lovely one), call me Mara, for the Almighty hath dealt very bitterly with me (Ruth 1.20). She needs the new name to describe her changed personality and chooses Mara, meaning bitter. Again Jacob called the heel-catcher (Gen. 25.26) after his encounter with God at Peniel changes his name to Israel at God's behest (Gen. 35.10). The writer indicates by the change of name a changed relationship.

The other side of this connection between a man and his name is illustrated in the feeling that the greatest disaster that could befall a Hebrew is that his name should be cut off. So Bildad describes the fate of the wicked: 'His roots dry up beneath, and his branches wither above. His memory perishes from the earth, and he has no name in the street' (Job 18.16-17). The name is an extension of the man's personality and every effort must be made to ensure its continuance for it is through his name that he may continue to live. (See Deut. 25.5f. for the practice of a man taking a dead brother's wife to continue the name of the deceased. This is called levirate marriage.)

The Name of the Lord as God himself. When we turn to the name of the Lord we find that in a number of contexts it is used for God himself. As a man's name is an extension of his very personality so is the Name of the Lord—*shem Yahweh*. Some examples will illustrate this characteristic usage. First, in the official Priestly blessing: 'The Lord bless thee and keep thee: The Lord make his face shine upon thee, and be gracious unto thee; the Lord lift up his countenance upon thee, and give thee peace. And they shall put my name upon the children of Israel; and I will bless them' (Num. 6.2-27). The comment in the last verse is significant with the parallelism of 'my name' and 'I'. The use of such parallel ideas in Hebrew support our understanding 'my name' as standing for God in person.

Psalm 20 is probably a liturgical composition and affords three examples of the use of the expression 'the name of the Lord' or 'the name of God'. In verse 1 we read: 'The Lord answer you in the day of trouble! The name of the God of Jacob protect you!' Further, in verse 5 we have, 'May we shout for joy over

your victory, and in the name of our God set up our banners!'
Finally, verse 7 reads, 'Some boast of chariots, and some of horses;
but we boast of the name of the Lord our God.'

The Deuteronomic Code also treats the Name of God as of
central significance. In chapter 12 there are three references to
this concept. So we read in verse 5: 'But you shall seek the place
which the Lord your God will choose out of all your tribes to
put his name there and make his habitation there' (see also vv. 11,
21 and 14.23-24; 16.6; 26.2). In these places God will himself
meet with his people. The Name of God represents God in person.

The Name of the Lord and worship. A further feature of the
use of the expression 'the name of the Lord' is in relation to the
act of worship. Thus we have such passages as, 'To Seth also a
son was born, and he called his name Enosh. At that time men
began to call upon the name of the Lord' (Gen. 4.26). Again in
the account of the journeyings of Abraham we read that he
'pitched his tent, with Bethel on the west and Ai on the east; and
there he built an altar to the Lord and called on the name of the
Lord' (Gen. 12.8, see also Zeph. 3.9). To call upon the name of
the Lord becomes a technical term for sharing in the services and
ritual of worship.

The Name of the Lord and God's relationship with his people.
In the thought of the ancient East to know a man's name meant
to have an intimate relationship with him. The knowledge of the
name gives a kind of power within this relationship. So it is with
God. When God answers the question of Moses as to his name
('What shall I say to them?') with the reply 'I am who I am', he
is not fobbing Moses off but is in a sense putting himself at the
disposal of Moses by revealing his name (Ex. 3.13-14). The dis-
closure of a name is tantamount to being willing to enter into
fellowship. This relationship is illustrated particularly well in
Ezekiel. We read in chapter 36 of the holy name of God: 'And
I will vindicate the holiness of my great name, which has been
profaned among the nations, and which you have profaned among

them; and the nations will know that I am the Lord, says the
Lord God, when through you I vindicate my holiness before their
eyes' (v.23,see also vv.20 and 22).The people have,through sin,
injured the relationship with God which the revelation of his
name, and so his nature, implies. Yet both in promise and in judgment the Lord is present in relation. These notes are heard in
such passages as: 'I will judge them; and they shall know that I
am the Lord' (Ezek. 7.27) and again, 'And I will stretch out my
hand against them, and make the land desolate and waste,
throughout all their habitations, from the wilderness to Riblah.
Then they will know that I am the Lord' (Ezek. 6.14). Yet God
is present with his people with promise too: 'And you shall know
that I am the Lord, when I open your graves, and raise you from
your graves, O my people' (Ezek. 37.13).

God is with his people to judge and to redeem. Such is his
nature and this he reveals when he discloses his name to men. To
know the name of the Lord is to be in fellowship with him, and
to walk in his name is to share in his purpose for his people. So
the Hebrew prophet bears his witness in an alien world: 'For
all the peoples walk each in the name of its god, but we will walk
in the name of the Lord our God for ever and ever' (Micah 4.5).

2 · The Holiness of God — *qadosh*

For may years the classic study of the meaning of holiness has
been *The Idea of the Holy* by Rudolf Otto. In this work he illustrates his theme again and again with reference to the mystery
and otherness of God in the Old Testament. He writes, 'Taken
in the religious sense, that which is "mysterious" is—to give it
perhaps the most striking expression—the "wholly other". The
Old Testament affords a striking example of God as the "Wholly
Other One" in such a passage as Hos. 11.9: "I will not execute
my fierce anger, I will not again destroy Ephraim; for I am God
and not man, the Holy One in your midst, and I will not come
to destroy." Perhaps the most notable passage is, of course, the
Inaugural Vision of Isaiah in chapter 6, the climax of which is

the cry of the seraphim: "Holy, holy, holy is the Lord of hosts; the whole earth is full of his glory (v. 3)." This vision dominates the life and ministry of the prophet.'

The word translated 'holy'—*qadosh*—and the way in which it is used indicate a number of characteristic features.

Holiness means separation from and separation for. In the Old Testament we find that an object or a person is sanctified, that is, made holy, and the meaning of such expressions is that they are separated from ordinary, everyday use and assigned to the service of God. God is the source of all that is holy. So in Gen. 14.7 we read of a place that is called Kadesh (*qadosh*). The verse reads: 'And they turned back and came to En-mishpat (that is Kadesh).' The phrase En-mishpat means 'a well of judgment'. Men came to a place called Kadesh to obtain an oracle or decision from God. The place is set apart for consulting God and so as a holy place is named Kadesh. So when the Old Testament speaks of a holy mountain (Isa. 11.9; Ezek. 20.40), a holy city (Joel 3.17) or a holy people (Deut. 7.6; Isa. 62.12), the central idea is that the mountain or city or people are the personal possession of God and are set apart for his service. They belong to God. Later because God is holy then of course people realized that if they were to belong to God they would have to be of the same nature and character. To be holy means not only a withdrawal from the ordinary everyday life but a positive dedication to the service of God. This means an involvement in the affairs of society. In two passages Isaiah shows the integral link between holiness and its moral consequence, that is righteousness: 'But the Lord of hosts is exalted in justice, and the Holy God shows himself holy in righteousness' (Isa. 5.11); again in Isaiah 30 we read, 'For they are a rebellious people, lying sons, sons who will not hear the instruction of the Lord; who say to the seers, "See not"; and to the prophets, "Prophesy not to us what is right; speak to us smooth things, prophesy illusions, leave the way, turn aside from

the path, let us hear no more of the Holy One of Israel" ' (vv.
9-11.

Holiness and the cult.   Holiness has a cultic and ritual aspect
as well as the inward and spiritual element. We find that holiness
is used as an equivalent to the idea of being ceremonially clean.
The Hebrew finds himself living in two worlds, the clean and the
unclean, the holy and the profane. In Amos 7.17 such categories
are applied to the land itself. The prophet in his judgment speaks
to Israel : 'You, yourself shall die in an unclean land.' The land
is unclean because it is a foreign land and not the land that belongs
to God. So the psalmist applies the term 'holy' to the centre of
all cultic activity, the Temple: 'Who shall ascend the hill of the
Lord? And who shall stand in his holy place?' (Ps. 24.3). The
vestments of the priests are holy (Lev. 16.4; Ex. 28.2); holy water
is used (Num. 5.17) and holy bread (I Sam. 21.6). The Ark of
the Lord must be placed in the most holy part of the sanctuary
(Ex. 26.34). On the Day of Atonement the priest must cleanse
himself, wear holy garments and even make atonement for the
holy place because of the uncleanness of the people of Israel (Lev.
16.4, 16, 23, 20). Holiness may therefore consist in scrupulous
obedience to cultic laws and the content of the term becomes cere-
monial purity. It is this cultic emphasis that we see in the passage
from Ezekiel which gives directions to the priests. 'And when
they go out into the outer court to the people they shall put off
the garments in which they have been ministering, and lay them in
the holy chambers; and they shall put on other garments, lest
they communicate holiness to the people with their garments'
(Ezek. 44.19). Here we have a return to the idea of holiness as
a physical contagion that could be transmitted. It is in this light
that we may best understand the incident of Uzzah who touches
the Ark of God: 'And the anger of the Lord was kindled against
Uzzah; and God smote him there because he put forth his hand
to the ark' (II Sam. 6.7). He is infected by the holiness of God

because he has come into contact with his holiness. (See also Ex. 19.12; Heb. 10.31 and I Sam. 6.)

Holiness involves communication. The Old Testament knows nothing about self-contained holiness. God who is holy is always thought as being in the midst of his people. Holiness represents a relationship as well as a quality. We find this illustrated especially in the use by Isaiah of the recurring title, the Holy One of Israel. So we read: 'For thus said the Lord God, the Holy One of Israel, In returning and rest you shall be saved; in quietness and trust shall be your strength' (Isa. 30.15; see also Isa. 10.20; 12.6; 17.7; 29.19). Behind this title, the Holy One of Israel, is the affirmation that God reveals and communicates his holiness, therefore his people must be holy too. 'And the Lord said to Moses, "Say to all the congregation of the people of Israel, You shall be holy; for I the Lord your God am holy" ' (Lev. 20.7; 21.8; 22.9, 31).

Holiness means redemption. A final characteristic of the use of holiness is the integral connection we find, in a number of passages in Deutero-Isaiah, with the act of redemption. We find this in the striking conjunction of the title 'the Holy One of Israel' with God's purpose of redeeming his people. So we read: 'Thus says the Lord, the Redeemer of Israel and his Holy One, to one deeply despised, abhorred by the nations, the servant of rulers: "Kings shall see and arise; princes, and they prostrate themselves; because of the Lord, who is faithful, the Holy One of Israel, who has chosen you" ' (Isa. 49.7, see also 41.14; 43.14; 48.17). So speaks God to one who is his servant in words that are akin to those Jesus used to describe his redemption of the world. (See also Isa. 52.13 and Isa. 53; Mark 10.45.) Holiness for the people of God must also include the redeeming of every sphere of our living, for we are holy to the Lord.

3 · **The Righteousness of God** — *tsedeq, tsedaqah, tsaddiq*
Are you a normal person? All readers of the Bible are con-

stantly meeting words that have this basic meaning of 'being normal'. The words are 'righteous' and 'righteousness' the usual translations of the Hebrew *tsaddiq* and *tsedeq* and *tsedaqah*. The fundamental idea is that of correspondence to a norm, which remains to be defined in every particular case. The central idea behind righteousness may be expressed in a number of ways.

Righteousness means correspondence to a norm. The norm may be material and physical. So in the Blessing of Moses he refers to the tribe of Zebulun in these words: 'Rejoice, Zebulun, in your going out, and Issachar in your tents. They shall call peoples to their mountains; there they offer right sacrifices' (Deut. 33.19). The original for 'right sacrifices' is 'sacrifices of righteousness' (see AV). The meaning is that they are the ones laid down in Hebrew law. In the well-loved twenty-third Psalm we have in v. 3 the phrase 'paths of righteousness' (AV). That is, paths that are straight not crooked. They conform to a straight line. From such examples of physical material norms we may turn to a moral norm. In Ps. 119.121 we have: 'I have done what is just and right, do not leave me to my oppressors.' The original for 'right' is *tsedeq*, that is the morally right thing to be expected has been done. The norm has been respected. (See also Job 35.2; Pss. 17.15; 45.8; Jer. 22.13.)

Righteousness involves social justice. In the story of Abraham's intercession on behalf of Sodom we find a further aspect of righteousness revealed in the association with social justice. God speaks: 'The Lord said, Shall I hide from Abraham what I am about to do, seeing that Abraham shall become a great and mighty nation, and all the nations of the earth shall bless themselves by him? No, I have chosen him, that he may charge his children and his household after him to keep the way of the Lord by doing righteousness and justice' (Gen. 18.17-19). The story contains the affirmation, 'Shall not the judge of all the earth do right?' (v. 25). God's judgment must always be righteous because he must always act in accordance with his own nature—this is his standard. Again we see the term applied to men and their carrying out the demands of the Laws which God has given for the community. In Deuteronomy 6 we read: 'And it will be righteousness for us, if we are careful to do all this commandment before the Lord our God, as he has commanded us' (v. 25).

Righteousness needs relationship. Men and God are called righteous in the Old Testament when there is an acknowledgment of their relationship. There is no basis for a man being righteous on his own. Solitary righteousness is a contradiction in terms. This is underlined in Ex. 9.27: 'Then Pharaoh sent, and called Moses and Aaron, and said to them, "I have sinned this time; the Lord is in the right (*tsaddiq*), and I and my people are in the wrong." ' The relationship between God and his worshippers is a relationship of 'being in the right'—that is, righteousness. The Egyptians and their Pharaoh are 'in the wrong' with God. The phrase 'in the right' brings out an essential note. The Hebrew form of the word comes from a verbal form meaning to cause to do right, that is, a man if he is righteous is always put in the right by God. The initiative is always with God.

In the well-known passage in Second Isaiah we have the affirmation: 'And there is no other god besides me, a righteous God a Saviour' (Isa. 45.21b). This has frequently been misunderstood as if there were a sort of tug-of-war in the mind and purpose of God, a tension between different parts of his nature. He would like to save men but he has to be just! The more profound way of looking at this passage is to see the salvation of the people as the outcome of his righteousness. It is because he is righteous that he will save. The righteousness of God is seen in the very act of saving the people. The righteous God is the loving God who pursues the salvation of his people and communicates his righteousness to the sinner and justifies him. This is the truth in Francis Thompson's *The Hound of Heaven*:

Halts by me that footfall:
Is my gloom, after all,
Shade of His hand, outstretched caressingly?

Righteousness presupposes faith. One of the great passages of
the New Testament throws further light on the biblical idea of
righteousness. This is Paul's testimony: 'But now the righteousness of God has been manifested apart from the law, although
the law and the prophets bear witness to it, the righteousness of
God through faith in Jesus Christ for all who believe . . . it was
to prove at the present time that he himself is righteous and that
he justifies him who has faith in Jesus' (Rom. 3.21-26). The word
translated 'justifies' comes from the same root as 'righteous' and
means 'to make righteous' or to 'put in the right'. This is what
God does—he acquits the guilty! This we have only to receive
in faith and we are righteous! The essential note in this passage
is that God's righteousness is not just an attribute of God. There
is a dynamic behind the Bible's idea of righteousness. Professor
Dodd has commented on the passage quoted above, 'the righteousness of God has been manifested' (v. 21) in these words: 'God
is now seen to be vindicating the right, redressing wrong, and
delivering men from the power of evil' (see *Moffatt Commentary
on Romans*, p. 13 and also p. 52).

To this saving activity of God who puts me in the right so that
I am righteous, I may respond by faith, and by faith alone.

4 · The Glory of God — *kabod*

We are familiar with the words of the Angel Song in Luke's
story of the birth of Christ: 'Glory to God in the highest, and
on earth peace among men with whom he is pleased' (Luke 2.14).
They summarize the whole purpose of our living, in church and
community. We seek to give glory to God. Every time we repeat
the doxology of the Lord's Prayer we express the same wish that
God might receive glory from men. What exactly do we mean?

The word *glory* is one of the key words of the Bible offering stimulus and challenge, as we examine the way in which it is used. The Old Testament word that we translate 'glory' is *kabod*, and the New Testament equivalent *doxa*. The original meaning of *kabod* is 'to be heavy or have weight'. It is used of both man and God and we shall look at these usages in turn.

In Ex. 29.13 the same root is used to describe a man's liver, that is, the heavy organ. Isa. 22.24 reads, 'And they will hang on him the whole weight of his father's house, the offspring and issue, every small vessel, from the cups to the flagons.' The word translated 'weight' in the R.S.V. is rendered 'glory' in the A.V. From the concept of physical weight the idea of *kabod* changes to that of wealth and so honour and majesty. We can see this illustrated in the protest of the sons of Laban against the sharp practice of Jacob when they say, 'Jacob has taken all that was our father's, he has gained all this wealth (*kabod*)' (Gen. 31.1). Similarly, the meaning of majesty and splendour is found in Ps. 21.5: 'His glory (*kabod*) is great through thy help; splendour and majesty thou dost bestow upon him.' We know that the Hebrews frequently wrote their poetry using parallel ideas rather than sounds that rhyme. Here 'glory' is equivalent to 'majesty and splendour'. We can almost see the loading of honours weighing a man down.

From the material sense of *kabod* as weight and wealth there is development to the non-physical ideas of honour and reputation and so glory and splendour as applied to men.

When we see the term glory applied to God we can distinguish a number of characteristic features in the way it is used.

The Glory of God offers guidance. There is a close link between the Glory of God and the act of seeing. The Glory of God is visible and so can act as a guide to the Israelites in their journeyings through the wilderness. 'At evening you shall know that it was the Lord who brought you out of the land of Egypt, and in the morning you shall see the glory of the Lord' (Ex. 16.6-7). Similarly, the Glory of God is seen when God gives the Tablets of the Law on Mount Sinai (Ex. 24.16) and after the completion of the Temple by Solomon when the priests come out of the Holy Place, the Temple is filled with the glory of the Lord (II Chron. 5.14). It is through his glory that God guides his people and reveals himself to them.

The Glory of God signifies the presence of God.   There are a number of passages where the term 'the glory of God' is clearly identical with God himself. In Isaiah chapter 6 the prophet described in his Call Vision the experience in the Temple and says emphatically that he saw the Lord. He continues with the picture of the seraphim crying one to another: 'Holy, holy, holy is the Lord of hosts; the whole earth is full of his glory' (Isa. 6.3). Yet in John's Gospel (12.41) the writer comments: 'Isaiah said this because he saw his glory and spoke of him.' Glory must mean that God reveals himself in person in a way that man can experience. The Glory of God means the presence of God. In the tragic days after the Ark of God had been captured and Eli dies through falling backward from his seat, his daughter-in-law, wife of Phinehas, gave birth to a son. Her naming of the child is symbolic: 'And she named the child Ichabod, saying, "The glory has departed from Israel, for the ark of God has been captured" ' (I Sam. 4.19-22). The Ark stood for the presence of God and since glory has gone God has gone. I-chabod is made up of an Hebrew negative and *kabod*—glory. (See Ezek. 9.3-4 for another example of glory meaning the presence of God.)

The Glory of God means the final victory of God.   The final characteristic of the way in which the concept of the glory of God is used is its close association with the ultimate victory of God's purposes. In the vision of the Herald Voices in Isaiah ch. 40, the climax of the spiritual experience of those in Exile is the cry, 'And the glory of the Lord shall be revealed, and all flesh shall see it together, for the mouth of the Lord has spoken' (v. 5). So Habakkuk during a time of questioning concerning the suffering of the good and the prosperity of the wicked affirms, 'For the earth shall be filled with the knowledge of the glory of the Lord as the waters cover the sea' (Hab. 2.14). For the individual, as for the nation, the Glory of God means victory. Thus in Psalm 73 the psalmist wrestles with the same problem as Habakkuk and reaches this insight: 'Nevertheless I am continually with thee; thou wilt hold my right hand. Thou dost guide me with thy counsel, and afterwards thou wilt receive me to glory (*kabod*)' (vv. 23-24). The psalmist is so near to God that any ultimate separation is inconceivable. Glory points the way to the Last Things and affirms that communion with God will go on after death. 'Faith overcomes death in the light of the eternal presence of God. It is God who guarantees the glory, and the life lived in communion with him is the basis on which this indestructible and victorious assurance of faith can become a living reality' (A. Weiser, *The Psalms*, 1962, p. 514).

In the New Testament, the idea of glory owed much to the Old Testament foundation. It is significant that the idea of glory is present in the accounts of the birth, crucifixion and the resurrection of Christ. We see this illustrated in the following passages. In the Prologue of John we read: 'The Word became flesh and dwelt among us, full of grace and truth; we beheld his glory, glory as of the only Son from the Father' (John 1.14). The climax of this Prologue is that men saw in the Incarnate Son the Glory of God, that is God himself revealed through his Son.

In the High Priestly Prayer of Jesus in John 17 we see Jesus facing the Cross. In the first ten verses we have six occurrences of the noun or verb 'glory' or 'glorify'. The Cross for Jesus was a matter of glory. Of course, this is because it was not defeat but triumph. As Cullmann has affirmed, the Cross was the dawning of D Day and the coming of V Day is assured (O. Cullmann, *Christ and Time*, 1951 and 1962, p. 84).

The central motif of glory is not missing from Paul's thought. For him glory and resurrection are inseparable: 'What is sown is perishable, what is raised is imperishable. It is sown in dishonour, it is raised in glory' (I Cor. 15.42-43; II Cor. 3.18; Phil. 3.21; Rom. 8.17, 21).

In the birth, the crucifixion and the resurrection of Christ we see the Glory of God and today in a fuller sense than possible in the days of the Old Testament, his glory guides us, represents God's presence in our midst and assures us of his ultimate victory.

5 · Covenant-Love — *chesed*

Our concern for this study is the word—*chesed*. It has been called 'the great sacramental word of the Old Testament Faith' (T. F. Torrance, *Scottish Journal of Theology*, 1948, p. 60). It is variously translated 'faithfulness, devotion, loving-kindness, steadfast love, leal-love or troth'. In each case some additional idea is added to that of love to save it from dilution and distortion.

The central meaning may be seen in such passages as Ps. 62.12-13:

> Once God has spoken;
> twice have I heard this:
> that power belongs to God;
> and that to thee, O Lord, belongs steadfast love,
> For thou dost requite a man according to his work.

In this passage we see that 'power' and 'steadfast love' are parallel, thus giving us the clue to the meaning of *chesed*—steadfast love. There is an underlying element of strength and power.

A further element in the meaning is found in the close association that we see between *chesed* and the word for faithfulness— *'emeth*. This is illustrated in Ps. 25.10 and Ps. 40.11:

All the paths of the Lord are steadfast love and faithfulness, for those who keep his covenant and his testimonies (Ps. 25.10).

I have not hid thy saving help within my heart,
I have spoken of thy faithfulness and thy salvation:
I have not concealed thy steadfast love and thy faithfulness from the great congregation (Ps. 40.11).

The pointer given by these passages is the fact that the word translated 'faithfulness' comes from the same root as the word for truth and our word 'Amen'. The picture is built up of an intensity and strength of emotion, akin to ardent zeal, that is all the time shown within a framework of relationship—hence the use of the phrase covenant-love. Here is no mere emotional feeling but a firm love directed to an expression of a strong resolute inner purpose—love with an inner stability. We may glance at some of the ways in which *chesed* is used.

Between man and man to represent a social bond. In the man to man relationships we see that the meaning of covenant-love is brought out. In Gen. 19.19 we have a picture of hospitality offered by Lot to his angel visitors and their advice to flee without a backward look. Yet he replies: 'Oh, no my lords; behold your servant has found favour in your sight, and you have shown me great kindness (*chesed*) in saving my life.' Behind this verse is the fellowship and social communion of the meal and *chesed* is used to describe the obligations that a shared meal implies. Again in II Sam. 10.2 we read: 'After this the king of the Ammonites died, and Hanun his son reigned in his stead. And David said, "I will deal loyally with Hanun the son of Nahash, as his father dealt loyally with me." ' The actual Hebrew for 'deal loyally' is 'to show *chesed*'.

Covenant-Love between God and man. The supreme illustration of the meaning of *chesed* is found in its use to describe how God deals with his people. Such a relationship is mirrored most significantly in the picture of the marriage bond that is the essence of Hosea's message. Here is a tale of heart-break. Imagine the feelings of Hosea, who after his marriage to Gomer, finds that his wife is unfaithful and the intimate sacrament of marriage is breaking up. Yet the miracle of this man's experience is that his love for his wife remains. Although he is not even sure that the children of his home are his own, in all his agony Hosea has one anchor—his abiding love for his wife. Whatever Gomer has done he cannot let her go. His personal anguish becomes a mirror for Hosea of God's relationship with Israel. If a man does not automatically lose his love even when the most intimate sanctities of marriage are desecrated, then how much more must God desire his people to return to him! There is no question of being let off. Behind Hosea's experiences we have the affirmation of covenant-love. God knows Israel even when she repents.

> Your love is like a morning cloud, like the dew that goes away early (6.4).

Yet God will bear the consequences of keeping to the covenant relationship.

> I will betroth you to me in righteousness and in justice, in stead-fast love (*chesed*) and mercy. I will betroth you to me in faithfulness; and you shall know the Lord (2.19).

Even after the Return from Exile we find the word *chesed* being used to describe the nation's struggles. The term is applied to those who remain true to the faith of their fathers and revere the Law. In times of persecution we read of the 'saints'—the devoted ones.

> Love the Lord, all you his saints!
> The Lord preserves the faithful, but abundantly requites him who acts haughtily (Ps. 31.28).

> Depart from evil, and do good: so shall you abide for ever. For the Lord loves justice; he will not forsake his saints (Ps. 37.27-8).

The word translated 'saints' in these passages comes from the same root as *chesed*—these are the ones who keep the covenant love.

In the times of the later Maccabean persecutions the custodians of the Law of God are called the *Chasidim*—the Devout—who preserve the integrity of Jewry in the second century BC as did their successors, the Pharisees, in AD 70 when the Temple was again destroyed. They all showed *chesed*—love within the Covenant.

The story reaches even to our own day in the discovery in 1947 of the writings called the Dead Sea Scrolls at Qumran. It is held as reasonable that the Covenanters of Qumran continued the heritage of witnessing to *chesed* in their belief that 'their faithfulness as the representative remnant of Israel would bring about a vicarious expiation for their nation and would help to usher in the new age of which the prophets had spoken' (D. S. Russell, *Between the Testaments*, 1960, p. 56).

So the word *chesed*—covenant-love—speaks of an abiding element in human experience, from the broken home of Hosea, the suffering of the martyrs who gave their lives in the Maccabean revolt to the Qumran Covenanters. They were all faithful to the demands of God's Covenant with his people.

6 · The Spirit of God — *ruach*

As we approach the story of Pentecost we meet a striking phrase in the account of Acts 2—'And suddenly a sound came from heaven like the rush of a mighty wind, and it filled all the house where they were sitting. And there appeared to them tongues as of fire, distributed and resting on each one of them. And they were all filled with the Holy Spirit and began to speak in other tongues, as the Spirit gave them utterance' (Acts 2.2-4). A sound like the rush of a mighty wind. The same connection between wind and Spirit is found in the account of the meeting between Jesus and Nicodemus by night. As the Lord speaks of the renewal of life for the individual he uses these words: 'The wind blows where it wills, and you hear the sound of it, but you do not know whence it comes or whither it goes; so it is with every one who is born of the Spirit' (John 3.8). The significant feature of these passages is that the same Greek word *pneuma* is used for both 'wind' and 'Spirit'. When we search the Old Testament we find that the same double role is played by *ruach*—both wind and spirit.

The original meaning of *ruach* (spirit) is 'air in motion', that is breath or wind. So in the delightful picture afforded by the Hebrew poet we see God walking in the garden in the cool (*ruach*) of the day—there is a slight breeze and it is chilly! (Gen. 3.8). As we examine the Old Testament usage of *ruach* we find a number of different affirmations made.

The Spirit reveals the nature of God's purpose. The Hebrews never separated the material from the spiritual but they claimed that the spiritual was expressed through the physical. Ultimately, God's purpose means the victory of the Spirit. In Isa. 31.3 we have a context that is familiar in our world, a struggle for a balance of power between nations. Israel at the cross-roads of the old civilizations is involved in power politics. Should she ally herself to Egypt against Assyria? The prophet reminds her that her real security is in God not in material resources: 'The Egyptians are men and not God; and their horses are flesh not spirit.' God's nature and his purpose are expressed through the Spirit. (See John 4.24.)

The Spirit offers dynamic power. A further characteristic of the use of *ruach* is the dynamic power that is associated with the Spirit's coming to man. Two examples will illustrate this. 'Then Samson went down with his father and mother to Timnah, and he came to the vineyards of Timnah. And behold, a young lion roared against him; and the Spirit of the Lord came mightily upon him and he tore the lion asunder as one tears a kid; and he had nothing in his hand' (Judg. 14.5-6). Here is dynamic power. Even more suggestive is the story of Gideon who is called by God to fight the battles of the Lord against the Midianites. The opposing forces of the Midianites and the Amalekites in league against Israel are encamped in the Valley of Jezreel. 'But the Spirit of the Lord took possession of Gideon; and he sounded the trumpet' (Judg. 6.34). The word translated 'took possession of' originally meant 'to put clothes on'. That means, the Spirit of God entered Gideon and put him on in the same way that Paul speaks of putting on the Lord Jesus Christ (Rom. 13.14). Wherever the Spirit comes to men he comes with power.

The Spirit means the difference between life and death. A number of passages in the Old Testament underline the difference that the presence or the absence of the Spirit means—the difference between life and death. So in Ps. 104.29-30 we read: 'When thou hidest thy face, they are dismayed; when thou takest away their breath, they die and return to their dust. When thou sendest forth thy Spirit (*ruach*) they are created; and thou renewest the face of the ground.' Again in the Vision of the Valley of Dry Bones in Ezekiel 37 we read: 'Thus says the Lord God to these bones: Behold I will cause breath to enter you and you shall live' (v. 5) and further in verse 16: 'And I will put my Spirit within you and you shall live.' The Spirit creates and sustains life (see Gen. 1.2). The presence of the Spirit makes all the difference between life and death.

The Spirit offers guidance. A further mark of the Spirit is the guidance that is offered to men and women who receive the Spirit. So the Psalmist cries: 'Teach me to do thy will, for thou art my God! Let thy spirit (*ruach*) lead me on a level path' (Ps. 143.10). The same note is sounded in the New Testament especially in the Gospel of John. In the group of Paraclete passages—this being the term used by him for the Spirit—three out of the five descriptions of the Paraclete are 'the Spirit of truth'. 'When the Spirit of truth comes, he will guide you into all the truth' (John 16.13, see also 14.17; 15.26).

The Spirit is personal, not a vague influence. The greatest insight of the Old Testament first and then the New Testament is that the Spirit means God himself in person not some indistinct shadowy influence. In the Bible the Spirit of God means himself. Thus in Ps. 139.7 we read: 'Whither shall I go from thy spirit (*ruach*); Or whither shall I flee from thy presence?' The words 'spirit' and 'presence' are equated. Similarly, in Psalm 51 the penitent cries: 'Cast me not away from thy presence and take not thy holy spirit from me' (v. 11). When the Bible speaks of the Spirit it means God in action personally. When we sing 'Come down, O Love Divine', this is the treasure we receive. We have power and guidance, vitality and, above all, the Presence of God.

> For none can guess its grace
> Till he become the place
> Wherein the Holy Spirit makes His dwelling.

7 · The Faithfulness of God — 'emeth, 'emunah

Through the Old Testament we find a recurring note—God is a God who can be trusted. He deals faithfully with Israel over and over again. A recent comment has been made on this integral connection of truth or trustworthiness with the nature of God: 'He may even be called the *God of the Amen*' (T. C. Vriezen, *An Outline of Old Testament Theology*, pp. 160-161). We shall look briefly at the insights that such a verdict contains.

Faithfulness means holding out. The Hebrew word for trustworthiness or faithfulness is 'emeth and it is used with the sense of 'to steady, to hold out'. Thus we find that the prophet Jeremiah describes the message of the false prophets:

Ah, Lord God, behold the prophets say to them, 'You shall not see the sword, nor shall you have famine, but I will give you assured peace in this place' (Jer. 14.13).

The phrase 'assured peace' literally reads 'peace of 'emeth'. The peace is thought to be a lasting, stable one. This note is reinforced by the cry of the psalmist:

The sum of thy word is truth ('emeth);
and every one of thy righteous ordinances endures for ever
(Ps. 119.160).

Again truth or trustworthiness ('emeth) is parallel to the concept of enduring for ever. There is the idea of stability, of holding on and holding out for ever.

Faithfulness means a relationship with God. A further feature of the way in which truth (*'emeth*) and faithfulness (*'emunah*) is used is the frequent linking of the two terms which are usually translated steadfast love and faithfulness—*chesed* and *'emunah*—to form a single idea of a union between God and man that is stable and enduring. In the account of the Sinai Covenant we read:

> The Lord, the Lord, a God merciful and gracious, slow to anger and abounding in steadfast love (*chesed*) and faithfulness (*'emeth*) (Ex. 34.6).

Again in the psalmist's exultant shout:

> Awake, O harp and lyre! I will awake the dawn ...
> For thy steadfast love is great to the heavens,
> Thy faithfulness to the clouds (Ps. 57.8-10).

The key to the thought is the relationship that is presupposed in the way that the words for truth and faithfulness are used by the Hebrew. The undertones of the idea of truth or trustworthiness are not those of an intellectual grasp of a satisfying accurate conclusion to an argument but relationship in covenant with a living God (see Hos. 2.21).

The God of the Amen. The verdict of Vriezen with which we started is expressed more fully in his translation of a passage in Isaiah:

> So that he who blesses himself in the land shall bless himself by the God of the Amen, and he who takes an oath in the land shall swear by the God of the Amen (Isa. 65.16).

The R.S.V. reads 'the God of truth' but the undertones of *'amen* and *'emeth* justify us in using the reading—the God of the Amen. We see the same process at work in the New Testament when Paul plays upon the meaning of the Amen in II Cor. 1.15-24:

> As surely as God is faithful, our word to you has not been Yes and No.... For all the promises of God find their Yes in him. That is why we utter the Amen through him, to the glory of God.

The word for faithfulness (*'emeth, 'emunah*) is connected in Hebrew with the word Amen and this forms the basis for Paul's speaking of Christ as the Amen of God.

Amen a triumphant verdict not a pious wish. The frequent understanding of *Amen* as a pious wistful wish—hoping it might be so—does less than justice to the teaching of the Bible. There is a central note of confidence and triumph in what the Bible means by *Amen.* In John's Gospel we find throughout the book the double phrase, 'truly, truly' as in John 3.3: 'Truly, truly, I say to you, unless one is born anew, he cannot see the kingdom of God.' The word translated 'truly' is the Greek equivalent of the Hebrew *'amen.* At the beginning of his affirmation Jesus says, this *is* so, not it *may* be so. We find in Deuteronomy 27 twelve occurrences of *'amen* as a signature of acceptance by the people of God's commandment. In the Book of Revelation we have the moving refrain uttered by the four living creatures around the throne of the Lamb:

> To him who sits upon the throne and to the Lamb be blessing and honour and glory and might for ever and ever! And the four living creatures said, Amen! and the elders fell down and worshipped (Rev. 5.14).

Amen is the guarantee that God gives of his faithfulness and of the ultimate victory of his purpose. The final Amen is Christ himself. So the Spirit says to the churches: 'And to the angel of the church in Laodicea write: "The words of the Amen, the faithful and true witness, the beginning of God's creation" ' (Rev. 3.14). Although the church community might be lukewarm, the outcome of the witness of the church is not in doubt, for the Amen has been spoken through Christ.

8 · The Blessing of God — *berakah*

One of the characteristics of the Ancient Near East, the world out of which the Old Testament came, is the tremendous power that was thought to reside in the spoken word. To our Western minds there is often a distinction made between what a man is and what he says. This is the very opposite to the Old Testament way of thinking—the word embodies the person and his purpose. There are two sides to this emphasis on the uttered word. The positive is called blessing and the negative called curse.

Blessing as word of power and dynamic. In such a passage as Deut. 30.1 we read:

And when all these things come upon you, the blessing and the curse which I have set before you. . . .

This is the crystallized choice before the Israelites as they face the Promised Land—they must choose life or death, blessing or curse. Again, this is the reason why, in the trick played upon the near-blind Isaac by Rebekah and Jacob, the blessing cannot be just cancelled. The wrong son has received the blessing but the words of blessing have gone forth and cannot be revoked. All that Isaac can do is to say, 'Who is it then who hunted game and brought it to me, and I ate it all before you came, and I have blessed him? . . . Yes, and he shall be blessed' (Gen. 27.33).

Blessing means the giving of life. In the usage of *barak* and *berakah*—to bless and blessing—we find a dominant theme is that blessing means the giving of life to man by God. In Genesis 1 we read of the fertility of both mankind and the animal world and they are directly connected with the gift of God's blessing. So we read, 'And God blessed them saying, Be fruitful and multiply and fill the waters of the seas, and let birds multiply on the earth' (Gen. 1.22). Similarly, after the creation of male and female we have: 'Be fruitful and multiply, and fill the earth and subdue it' (v. 28).

A further example of the association between blessing and the giving of life and fertility is found in Psalm 84:

Blessed is he whose strength is in thee,
when he meditates in his heart on pilgrimages.

As they pass through the valley of tears,
they make it a place of springs,
a place of blessing such as the early rain imparts (vv. 5-6, trans.
Weiser).

The blessedness of the devout pilgrim, so the poet believes, is such
that the fatigue of pilgrimage with all its hardships is like passing
through the valley of tears 'which the pilgrims transform into a
place of springs ... even the bleak steppe becomes for him a
landscape with bubbling fountains and pasture, which the early
rain, ardently hoped for after the long spell of summer heat, trans-
forms from a desert into fields richly blessed with fruit' (Weiser,
pp. 565, 567). Here is the blessing of God seen in the fertility
and is the sign of God-given life to the land and so to the be-
lieving people.

Blessing and the face of God.   A further element in the use of
blessing (*berakah*) is the close association between receiving a
blessing and the face of God. This link is seen in the following
passages.

First, in the blessing that God tells Moses to pronounce upon
the people of Israel.

Thus shall you bless the people of Israel: you shall say to them,
The Lord bless you and keep you:
The Lord make his face to shine upon you,
and be gracious to you:
The Lord lift up his countenance upon you
and give you peace (Num. 6.23-26).

This is far more than a pious wish; it is the setting in motion of
an actual beneficent power, for they have been in the presence
of God and his face has looked upon them for good. The psalmist
repeats this idea when he utters three times the refrain:

Restore us, O God;
let thy face shine, that we may be saved (Ps. 80.3, 7, 19).

Here is life's richest blessing that God's face shall turn towards his children in love. In the practice of the presence of God is blessing.

Blessing is no monopoly for a select nation. When Abraham was called by God into a covenant relationship, the intention of God was not to exalt the Israelites into a position of privilege but rather of responsibility. The blessing that comes to an elect people will itself be the very means by which the whole creation shall be blessed. So we read:

> And I will make you a great nation, and I will bless you, and make your name great, so that you will be a blessing ... and by you all the families of the earth will be blessed
>
> (Gen. 12.3; see also 22.18; 26.4; 28.14).

In this call to Abraham the same word—*barak*, to bless—is used five times. This is the dominant note that God must communicate. He wants to bless his chosen people as a way of blessing the world in its entirety. Blessing from the outset of the Bible story is not national or local in its purpose but universal.

Blessing we have seen means real power, active in human life, the means by which God grants abundant life. Its fullest expression is the outcome of being near enough to God that his face shall shine upon us and through us upon those who are afar off, even to the ends of the earth. What can a man say in response to the blessing of God other than to echo the words of the psalmist:

> Bless the Lord, O my soul!
> and all that is within me,
> bless his holy name!
> Bless the Lord, O my soul,
> and forget not all his benefits (Ps. 103.1-2).

9 · The Kingship of God — *melek, malkuth*

God is king! This is the meaning of the cry of the psalmist when he proclaims: The Lord reigns; let the earth rejoice! (Ps. 97.1 and Pss. 93.1; 99.1). We do not find the phrase 'Kingdom of God's used in the Old Testament but the concept is certainly there and in this study we shall look at the usage of the Hebrew words *melek* (king) and *malkuth* (kingdom) that we might the better appreciate all that Jesus meant by his teaching concerning the *basileia*—the kingdom—in the New Testament.

The role of king. The Hebrew word *melek* is the one used for the office of king and as we examine the function of the *melek* we find that his role is primarily three-fold:

The king as saviour of the nation in war. He is the leader of the nation in battle and we must remember that the wars of Old Testament times were always the wars of the Lord. They were sacred activities rather than mere military exploits. So we read in Judg. 7.18: 'When I blow the trumpet, I and all who are with me, then blow the trumpets also on everyside of all the camp, and shout, "For the Lord and for Gideon." ' Gideon was fighting the battles of the Lord. Further in Judg. 3.9 we have, 'But when the people of Israel cried unto the Lord, the Lord raised up a deliverer for the people of Israel, who delivered them.' Thus the Bible writers saw the work of Othniel against the king of Mesopotamia rather than just another skirmish between warring tribes.

The king as the dispenser of justice. A second part of the royal function was to administer justice and especially to safeguard the rights of the individual. So we read in the prophecy of Isaiah: 'For unto us a child is born, to us a son is given; and the government will be upon his shoulder and his name will be called "Wonderful Counsellor, Mighty God, Everlasting Father, Prince of Peace". Of the increase of his government and of peace there will be no end, upon the throne of David, and over his kingdom, to establish it, and to uphold it with justice and with righteousness from this time forth and for evermore.' (Isa. 9.6-7; see also Isa. 11.1-5; 16.5; Jer. 33.15; Prov. 16.10.)

The king as mediator between God and man. The king (*melek*) has a double part to play as the representative of God to the people and as the representative of the people before God. This is illustrated in the following passages which underline the endowment of the Spirit that he receives for his task. 'Then Samuel took the horn of oil, and anointed him in the midst of his brethren, and the Spirit of the Lord came mightily upon David from that day forward' (I Sam. 16.13). In the Psalter we have such a passage as Ps. 2.4-7: 'He who sits in the heavens laughs; the Lord has them in derision. Then he will speak to them in his wrath, and terrify them in his fury, saying, "I have set my king on Zion my holy hill." I will tell of the decree of the Lord: He said to me, "You are my son, today I have begotten you." ' It is this last verse that coupled with Isa. 42.1, is the basis of the testimony from heaven at the Baptism of Jesus—'This is my beloved Son, with whom I am well pleased' (Matt. 3.17). Another passage containing reference to the king as the spokesman of God is Ps. 45.6-7, where the king is addressed in what was originally a royal marriage song: 'Your divine throne endures for ever and ever. Your royal sceptre is a sceptre of equity; you love righteousness and hate wickedness. Therefore, God, your God, has anointed you with the oil of gladness above your fellows.' The king holds his power as from God but he must wield it on behalf of the people. In all these passages a central principle is affirmed. The king in Hebrew thought is no Eastern potentate ruling with arbitrary and despotic power. He is the Anointed of the Lord and committed to the service of the Lord's people. The rule of the king is to be the rule of God.

The kingship of God.   As we turn from *melek* (king) to *melkuth* (kingdom or kingship), we look at two passages containing this word. In Psalm 22 we read: 'All the ends of the earth shall remember and turn to the Lord; and all the families of the nations shall worship before him. For dominion (*malkuth*) belongs to the Lord and he rules over the nation' (vv. 27-28). The meaning of *malkuth* here is more kingship than any idea of territory. The psalmist is expressing the universal sovereignty of God. Again in

Psalm 145 we have: 'All thy works shall give thanks to thee, O Lord, and all thy saints shall bless thee! They shall speak of the glory of thy kingdom, and tell of thy power to make known to the sons of men thy mighty deeds, and the glorious splendour of thy kingdom. Thy kingdom is an everlasting kingdom, and thy dominion endures throughout all generations' (vv. 10-13). The resounding note is that of the majesty and power of the kingship of God. It is this use of *malkuth* that prepares us for the New Testament phrase, the Kingdom of God and the interpretation of it as the kingship or rule of God that all men may accept here and now.

The kingdom and the saints. The final aspect of the Old Testament teaching concerning the Kingdom is found in the Book of Daniel. 'But the saints of the Most High shall receive the kingdom, and possess the kingdom for ever, for ever and ever' (7.18). The word translated 'saints' means the 'holy ones'. These are the men and women who have known the full violence of the Maccabean persecutions and tortures yet through a leap of faith believe that the Kingdom of God will be given them. The Kingdom is not of this world, another empire, but the rule of God for ever and ever. This Kingdom is of his gift, both here and now in the acceptance of his rule and yet in its fullest consummation the saints of every land and age will know its wonder. The original meaning of 'holy ones' is 'those who belong to God'. It is within this relationship of belonging to him that the Kingdom comes.

10 · The Face of God — *panim 'Elohim*

One of the features of Hebrew thought is the emphasis laid again and again upon the parts of the human body, such as the eyes, hand, arm and internal organs. These are used to bring out the variety of feelings and attitudes of mind of the person in different situations. Of especial significance is the face—*panim*. So in Ps. 104.15 we have reference to the face of a man and his feeling of joy and gladness—'and wine to gladden the heart of man, and to make his face shine, and bread to strengthen man's heart' (see also Prov. 15.13). In Gen. 4.5, the offering of Cain is rejected, 'so Cain was very angry and his face (*panim*) fell' (see also Neh. 2.2). In one passage we have three idiomatic expressions all using the word *panim*—face. The context is the encounter between Jacob and Esau after the years of estrangement. Jacob's conflict of mind is described: 'For he thought, "I may appease him with the present that goes before me and afterwards I shall see his face; perhaps he will accept me"' (Gen. 32.21). The Hebrew for 'appease' is literally 'I will cover his face' and 'will accept me' is 'Lift up my face'. The face—*panim*—is clearly in various moods an index of human personality.

The face of God as God in person. Not only is the face used of man as an indication of the man's personality but also the Old Testament speaks frequently of the face of God. We may look at three examples in differing contexts. The first scene is at the Tent of Meeting, the rendezvous of God with Moses. 'Thus the Lord used to speak to Moses face to face as a man speaks to his friend' (Ex. 33.11). So Moses claiming the right of this intimacy demands that God shows him his future plans in this difficult wilderness situation. To this request of a friend, God replies: 'And he said, "My presence will go with you and I will give you rest." And he said to him, "If thy presence (*panim*) will not go with me, do not carry us up from here"' (Ex. 33.14-15). The word translated 'presence' is actually face. The 'face of God' is clearly understood as God himself in the midst of his people without reservation.

Again in Deut. 4.37 we have an interpretation of God's deliverance of the Israelites from Egypt: 'And because he loved your fathers and chose their descendants after them, and brought you out of Egypt with his own presence (*panim*), by his great power. . . .' The phrase 'his own presence' is literally 'with his face'. The whole emphasis of the passage is that God himself had delivered them, not an intermediary.

A third context is provided in the Psalter. The writer describes in turn the situation of the king and then his enemies. 'Yea, thou dost make him most blessed for ever; thou dost make him glad with the joy of thy presence (*panim*)' (Ps. 21.6); then follows, 'Your hand will find out all your enemies; your right hand will find out those who hate you. You will make them as a blazing oven when you appear' (vv. 8-9).

The word 'face' is used in both cases. The last phrase 'when you appear' is literally 'the time of your face', that is a reference to the personal intervention of the Lord himself.

The face of God as a revelation of himself.   In the variety of ways and contexts in which the phrase 'the face of God' appears there is a central feature that is never absent. The 'face of God' is always a revelation of his nature and his purpose. We find, for example, the phrase 'seek the face of the Lord' used as a way of expressing the aim of both the Temple's cultic rites and also the profound prayer of the individual. So we read in Psalm 63: 'O God, thou art my God, I seek thee, my soul thirsts for thee; my flesh faints for thee as in a dry and weary land where no water is. So I have looked upon thee in the sanctuary, beholding thy power and glory' (vv. 1-2). The use of the verb 'looked upon thee' and 'beholding', although not using the actual word for 'face', certainly presupposes the same concept. The actual word is used by another psalmist in Psalm 17: 'As for me, I shall behold thy face in righteousness; when I awake I shall be satisfied with beholding thy form' (v. 15). In Psalm 95 the privilege of corporate worship is referred to with deep gratitude: 'O come, let us sing unto the Lord; let us make a joyful noise to the rock of our salvation! Let us come into his presence (*panim*) with thanksgiving; let us make a joyful noise to him with songs of praise!' (vv. 1-2). Thus in the worship of the Temple as part of the cult and in the individual approach to God we find that men seek the face of the Lord to know his will and purpose.

The face of God and communion with man. A final element in the usage of the phrase 'the face of God' is that of communion between God and man. In a number of passages in the law codes we read: 'All the first-born of your sons you shall redeem. And none shall appear (originally "shall see me") empty' (Ex. 34.20; see Deut. 16.16; Ex. 23.15). The original expression about seeing God is retained in Ex. 24.11: 'And he did not lay his hand on the chief men of the people of Israel; they beheld God and ate and drank.' The original sense of direct encounter is also retained in Ps. 42.2: 'When shall I come and behold the face of God?' In a more intimate way we read in Psalm 27: 'Hear, O Lord, when I cry aloud, be gracious to me and answer me! Thou hast said, "Seek ye my face." My heart says to thee, "Thy face, Lord, do I seek." Hide not thy face from me' (vv. 7-9). If the face of God represents communion and blessing (see Study 8), to be alienated from God is expressed in the opposite way. It is the dread experience to be feared above all, that God should hide his face. In the prophecy of Deutero-Isaiah we read: 'For a brief moment I forsook you, but with great compassion I will gather you. In overflowing wrath for a moment I hid my face from you, but with everlasting love I will have compassion on you, says the Lord, your Redeemer' (Isa. 54.7-8). (See also Deut. 31.17; 32.20; Isa. 59.2; 64.6; Jer. 33.5; Ezek. 33.23.)

The experience of the human race is crystallized in the picture of Cain's condemnation to be a fugitive, away from the face of God: 'Behold, thou hast driven me this day away from the ground; and from thy face I shall be hidden' (Gen. 4.14) Such is our common lot until we return to seek his face, for with the psalmist we would cry, 'when thou hidest thy face, they are dismayed; when thou takest away their breath, they die and return to their dust' (Ps. 104.29).

11 · **The Fear of the Lord** — *yir'ath Yahweh*

The very sound of this familiar phrase conjures up for many a picture of a God who is a tyrant, despotic and arbitrary in his dealings with men. In this brief study we shall seek to correct this negative, one-sided picture and present the positive affirmations that lie behind this expression.

The original Hebrew is *yir'ath Yahweh* and is used frequently in the Old Testament with a wealth of meaning. The full riches of the phrase may be better appreciated as we consider three affirmations.

The fear of the Lord is the other side of communion.   One of the great characteristics of the nature of the Lord (Yahweh) is that he is not a God remote from his people. He visits them, he is Immanuel—God with us (Isa. 7.14). Yet the idea of communion is part of a double concept. God is such that he has communion with man but man knows himself unworthy of being in the presence of God. The two elements are kept in tension—the holiness of God and his communion with man. Both are needed to express the way that God comes to man and the way that man feels when he does come. This is the first usage of the phrase 'the fear of the Lord'. It keeps the balance between holiness and communion. Man must not become too familiar with God. Rather he reacts in God's presence as the prophet Isaiah did: 'Woe is me! For I am lost; for I am a man of unclean lips, and I dwell in the midst of a people of unclean lips; for mine eyes have seen the King, the Lord of Hosts!' (Isa. 6.5). Or again we remember Jeremiah with his humility as he is commissioned by God: 'Ah, Lord God! Behold, I do not know how to speak, for I am only a youth' (Jer. 1.6; see also Ex. 6.30 and Ezek. 1.28 for the similar reactions of Moses and Ezekiel).

The fear of the Lord involves the knowledge of God.   A second feature of the way in which 'the fear of the Lord' is used is its relationship to another great biblical expression—the knowledge of God (*da'ath 'Elohim*, see Study 16 below). We find these two expressions as parallels in such passages as: 'And the Spirit of the Lord shall rest upon him, the spirit of wisdom and understanding, the spirit of counsel and might, the spirit of knowledge and the fear of the Lord. And his delight shall be in the fear of the Lord' (Isa. 11.2).

The psalmist reinforces the parallel: 'The fear of the Lord is the beginning of wisdom' (Ps. 111.10) as does the sage when he writes, 'The fear of the Lord is the beginning of knowledge' (Prov. 1.7) and further, 'The fear of the Lord is the beginning of wisdom, and the knowledge of the Holy One is insight' (Prov. 9.10).

In these last three passages we must note that the Hebrew expression 'the beginning of' (Hebrew *rosh*—head) does not mean a mere introduction to wisdom or knowledge in these contexts but that the fear of the Lord is both foundation and consummation. The Lord is Alpha and Omega (Rev. 21.6) and to fear the Lord is the initiation of the good life, the only way to start, and further, the very goal itself. To fear the Lord means that the Lord reveals himself to us and in the relationship that knowledge brings we commit ourselves to him.

The fear of the Lord as life's dominant motive. The final element in the use of the expression 'the fear of the Lord' is seen especially in the Book of Proverbs. In this work the choice between good and evil, life or death, is put forcibly before the youth of the nation. The whole work is an attempt to gain allegiance to God by the 'don't knows' of the day. The search for wisdom means not intellectual curiosity but committal to a way of life. Throughout this early attempt to sway the thinking of the youth of the day we see that the writers are dominated by one master concept, which is the dynamic behind their concern for the good life. This concept is 'the fear of the Lord'. It is through the fear of the Lord that one is brought to hate evil (Prov. 3.7; 8.13). The fear of the Lord prolongs life (10.27) and gives new confidence (14.26). The fear of the Lord is a fountain of life (14.27) and the sage concludes 'The fear of the Lord leads to life' (19.23). This is the contemporary and recurring choice—life or death! In effect, 'the fear of the Lord' comes to mean all that we intend by using the terms 'religion' and 'religious faith'. Theodore Robinson has commented, ' "The Fear of Yahweh" then sums up in itself the attitude which the religious man will assume towards the object of his worship; as has been well said, it is, perhaps, the nearest phrase in Hebrew to that which we call "religion" ' (*The Poetry of the Old Testament*, 1947, p. 169).

The fear of the Lord stands not for terror but truth. The truth that comes to those who have been given knowledge of God and as a result have given every energy and power they have in his service. In this practice of real religion they have known the communion with God that the very fear of God brings.

II

CONCERNING MAN

In this section we look at some of the insights contained by words that describe the response of man to the acts of God. It is not too much to say that it is through the responses of man that we gain our knowledge of how God himself acts. It is this principle of seeing man's response as a guide to God's nature that is embodied in the greatest act of God—his becoming Man. If we would know how God acts we must see how man reacts. Full knowledge comes only from the relationship between God and his creature man. Here is the heart of the Gospel of the Incarnation.

12 · **The Word** — *dabar*

In the modern Western world we tend to separate a man's words from his deeds. Actions, we say, speak louder than words. Yet in the world from which the Bible came, a much richer significance is seen in the words of a man and especially in the words uttered by God. The Hebrew word that is usually translated 'word' is *dabar* and in this study we shall seek to find some part of the fundamental importance of the word for biblical interpretation.

The two uses of dabar. There are two main senses in which *dabar* is used: first, to represent speech or utterance and secondly, with the meaning of thing or matter. So we find in Ex. 20.1: 'And God spoke all these words (*debarim*) saying. . . .' We have been accustomed to call the passage following the account of the Ten Commandments but the original means 'the Ten Words' that have been uttered by God. This use of *dabar* to stand for a communication involving the act of speaking is the most frequent one. However, in a number of passages such a translation as 'word' would not suit the context. So in Exodus 5 we read of the oppression of the Egyptian taskmasters and their insistence that the Israelites make bricks without straw: 'Complete your work, your daily task, as when there was straw' (v.13). The phrase 'daily task' is literally the *dabar* of a day. Again in the story of Saul looking for the lost donkeys of his father we read: 'And Saul said to his uncle, "He told us plainly that the asses has been found." But about the matter (*dabar*) of the kingdom, of which Samuel has spoken, he did not tell him anything' (I Sam. 10.16; also I Sam. 21.9). Of particular interest is the passage in Ezekiel: 'And the word of the Lord came to me: "Son of man, what is this proverb that you have about the land of Israel, saying, 'The days grow long, and every vision comes to naught'? Tell them therefore, 'Thus says the Lord God: I will put an end to this proverb, and they shall no more use it as a proverb in Israel.' But say to them, The days are at hand, and the fulfilment of every vision. . . . But I the Lord will speak the word which I will speak, and it will be performed. It will be no longer be delayed, but in your days, O rebellious house, I will speak the word and perform it, says the Lord God"' (Ezek. 12.22-25). The word translated 'fulfilment' is better rendered 'the subject-matter of the vision' and it is '*dabar*'. In this instance, not only is the *dabar* uttered or spoken but the Lord God will perform it. The word becomes the thing which happens, the event. Similarly, we find *dabar* used with the meaning of 'event, happening' in such passages as I Kings 14.19: 'Now the acts of Rehoboam, and all that he did are they not written in the Book of the Chronicles of the Kings of Judah?' The word that is translated 'Chronicles' is the plural of *dabar* and here certainly means a daily record of events kept in some royal archives (see also II Chron. 33.18). A further use of *dabar* with the sense of event is found in the frequently recurring opening phrase 'after these things'. 'After these things the word of the Lord came to Abram in a vision' (Gen. 15.1; see also Gen. 22.1; I Kings 17.17; Ezra 7.1; Esth. 2.1). The meaning in these passages being 'event in time'.

The word and its power. A feature of the use of *dabar* is its association with the dynamic of power. Once a word is uttered it can exert an influence for good or evil. We have already seen special cases of this belief in the significance attached to the name of the Lord and the ideas of blessing and curse. We find a well-known passage in Deutero-Isaiah that illustrates the power of the word: 'For as the rain and snow come down from heaven, and returns not thither but waters the earth, making it bring forth and sprout, giving seed to the sower and bread to the eater, so shall my word be that goes forth from my mouth; and it shall not return to me empty, but it shall accomplish that which I purpose, and prosper in the thing for which I sent it' (Isa. 55.10-11). The same idea of a creative word is implicit in the account of creation in Genesis 1 where different phases of creation are prefaced with 'And God said' (see vv. 3, 6, 9, 14, 20, 24 and 26). Similarly, the psalmist affirms the power of the word when he cries: 'By the word of the Lord the heavens were made, and all their host by the breath of his mouth' (Ps. 33.6).

The word of God as God in person. In a number of passages we have a further characteristic of the use of *dabar*. That is, the equation of the word of God with God himself. This understanding of *debar Yahweh*—the word of the Lord—underlies the whole prophetic writings. In the accounts of God's commissioning his prophets we find repeatedly such words as: 'Now the word of the Lord came to me saying, "Before I formed you in the womb I knew you, and before you were born, I consecrated you; I appointed you a prophet to the nations"' (Jer. 1.4-5). The expression 'the word of the Lord came' is another way of saying that God himself came to the prophet and chose him to do his work. See also the same description of the call given to Jonah (Jonah 1.1), Micah (Micah 1.1) and Hosea (Hos. 1.1). Here in these encounters God is present in his word. Thus early in Hebrew thought we see the unfolding of his purpose. The fuller gospel is already implicit in the concept of the Word that comes to man, the Word that is God. The commissioning involves communion with God himself.

The Word becomes flesh.   Through the use of *dabar* as both word and thing and the further use of the Word of the Lord to represent God himself, we are prepared for the climax of the biblical use of *dabar* found in the pages of the New Testament through the use of *Logos*. In the Prologue of John we read: 'And the Word became flesh and dwelt among us, full of grace and truth; we have beheld his glory, glory as of the only Son from the Father' (John 1.14). Here is the Living Word in the person of the Living Lord. God's speaking and his acting are one. God's final word is incarnate in a person, not a proposition.

13 · The Soul and the Self — *nephesh*

In Hebrew psychology one of the great words providing the key to what we now call the soul or even the self is the word *nephesh*. The term personality is comparatively modern but *nephesh* includes all that we mean by it. It is the word that is translated in the New Testament by *psyche* from which the term psychology comes. We find three main groups of ideas associated with the word *nephesh*.

Nephesh *and the breath of life.*   In Isa. 5.14 we have a picture of Sheol, the Hebrew world of the dead, personified as some devouring monster widening her throat for its victims: 'Therefore Sheol enlarged its appetite and opened its mouth beyond measure.' The word translated 'appetite' is *nephesh*. Similarly, in the Book of Jonah we read in Jonah's prayer: 'The waters closed in over me, the deep was round about me' (2.5). The actual Hebrew for 'closed in over me' is 'were right up to the *nephesh*'. That is, up to his neck or throat. This indicates his extreme danger. The word is thus associated with the throat and neck. The story of God breathing into the nostrils of the man he had formed from the dust reads, 'Then the Lord God formed man from of dust from the ground, and breathed into his nostrils the breath of life; and man became a living being (*nephesh*)' (Gen. 2.7). As the word is used of the creation of life so it is used of its restoration. In the Book of Ruth 4.15 we have the following passage: 'Blessed be the Lord, who has not left you this day without next of kin; and may his name be renowned in Israel! He shall be to you a restorer of life and a nourisher of your old age.' So the women speak to Naomi of the child that Ruth bears to Boaz. The original for 'restorer of life' is 'one who brings back the *nephesh*'.

Nephesh *as the seat of desire, mood and purpose.* There is a clear relation between the use of *nephesh* and the expression of a person's desire, mood or central purpose. In Hosea we have a scathing indictment of the priests and their neglect of their sacred task. The prophet bursts out: 'They feed on the sin of my people; they are greedy for their iniquity' (Hos. 4.8). The literal rendering of 'they are greedy for' is 'they lift up their *nephesh*'. That is the picture before the prophet of the strong, panting breath of desire for evil of those who batten on a vicious, decadent system of religious ritual divorced from right living. In another mood we feel the deep emotion contained in the Servant Song of Deutero-Isaiah: 'He shall see the fruit of the travail of his soul and be satisfied' (Isa. 53.11). Here *nephesh* is translated 'soul' and clearly carries the meaning of deep spiritual emotion. A final example in this second group of meanings is found in II Kings 9.15 where we have an account of the anointing of Jehu as King of Israel. After he has been acclaimed by the trumpets of the people and given the commission of killing Jezebel he commands, 'If this is your mind, then let no one slip out of the city to go and tell the news in Jezreel.' The Hebrew reads 'if this is your *nephesh*', that is if this is your mind and purpose that I should be king.

Nephesh *as soul or personality.* The word is also used to express personality, both individual and corporate, and is sometimes translated by the first person pronoun, I. The wilderness experience of the Israelites affords a good example of the corporate use of *nephesh*. The scene is one of protest against the rigorous conditions. They have short-lived memories and attack Moses with the words: 'Why have you brought us up out of Egypt to die in the wilderness? For there is no food and no water, and we loathe this worthless food' (Num. 21.4). The translation 'we loathe' barely does justice to the original which is 'our *nephesh* is sick of this food.' The one *nephesh* is used to describe the corporate personality of the whole people. A familiar usage for the individual self is found in the account of the Passover: 'On the first day you shall hold a holy assembly, and on the seventh day a holy assembly; no work shall be done on those days; but what every one must eat, that only may be prepared by you' (Ex. 12.16). 'Every one' translates every *nephesh* that is, every person or individual. Again, in Isaiah we have the impassioned outburst: 'Your new moons and your appointed feasts my soul hates; they have become a burden to me, I am weary of bearing them' (Isa. 1.14). The phrase 'my soul' renders 'my *nephesh*' and could equally well be 'I detest'. This is God speaking in the first person.

We have seen that *nephesh* may variously mean throat or breath of life, desire, emotion or purpose, and personality, individual or corporate, the self or the soul. Here is a key to the New Testament use of *psyche*—soul. The body and soul of man are not to be treated separately as distinct. The use of *nephesh* prepares us for seeing man as body-soul. We are prepared for the very affirmation of the Incarnation. Man is 'an animated body and not an incarnated soul.' The dualism of much later thought between form and matter is not found in the Bible. Man is a *nephesh* and the word covers the whole of man—his soul and his self.

14 · The Heart — *leb*

We have seen in a previous study of 'the face of God' that a characteristic of Hebrew thought is the frequent use of parts of the physical body to represent inner emotions and feelings and to speak of one physical part of the organism when meaning the whole personality. The present study seeks to sketch although briefly the different ways in which the Old Testament uses the word *leb*—heart.

The whole trend of the use of *leb* is away from the understanding of heart as a predominantly emotional or affectional word which is largely the meaning of the word to Western readers. In varying contexts the will and purpose, the mind and the whole personality may be meant when *leb* is used.

Heart as the seat of emotion. We find that *leb* is used of emotional response to a situation in a number of different ways. It is used of joy and gladness, as in Ruth 3.7: 'And when Boaz has eaten and drunk and his heart was merry, he went to lie down at the end of the heap of grain.' In Eccles. 7.3 sorrow forms part of the heart's response: 'Sorrow is better than laughter for by sadness of countenance the heart is made glad.' Again in the psalmist's plaint fear is the dominant emotion in such a passage as Ps. 22.14: 'I am poured out like water, and all my bones are out of joint; my heart is like wax, it is melted within my breast.'

Heart as mind and will. The main emphasis when the Hebrews speak of the heart of a man is upon the intellect and the will, not the emotions. We see this in the following passages. First, the prophet Hosea speaks of the nation that will still persist in putting her trust in political alliances with Egypt or Assyria rather than relying upon her God: 'Ephraim is like a dove, silly and without sense, calling to Egypt, going to Assyria' (Hos. 7.11). The Hebrew for 'without sense' is 'without *leb* (heart)'. The meaning is that Ephraim is not using any judgment of mind at all, she is not behaving sensibly rather than behaving without feeling. Again in the teaching of the Sages we read: 'Then I saw and considered it; I looked and received instruction' (Prov. 24.32). Literally the translation 'considered it' is 'set my heart upon it'. This is a direct parallel to our own way of speaking, in the phrase, 'I put my mind to it.'

The resolution of will and purpose is seen when the psalmist affirms: 'I believe that I shall see the goodness of the Lord in the land of the living! Wait for the Lord; be strong, and let your heart (*leb*) take courage' (Ps. 27.14). Again, in the appearing of God to Job at the close of the cycle of speeches, he speaks of his power: 'His heart is hard as a stone, hard as the nether millstone' (Job 41.24). The reference is to Leviathan, probably an echo of the primeval chaos monster. All the time the omnipotence of God is being urged upon Job. In the picture-language used, the heart is described as having the iron resolution of purpose rather than any emotional feeling.

The heart as representing the whole man.   As well as sometimes expressing emotion or mind and will, 'heart' (*leb*) in a number of passages represents the whole man, all that we mean by the complete rounded personality, the man himself. So in Gen. 17.17 when Abraham is told by God that Sarah will bear a son: 'Then Abraham fell on his face and laughed, and said to himself, "Shall a child be born to a man who is a hundred years old?"' The Hebrew for 'to himself' is 'in his *leb*'. The heart may here represent the whole man. Again, the psalmist speaks of evil men who have rejected God: 'He thinks in his heart (*leb*), God has forgotten, he has hidden his face, he will never see it' (Ps. 10.6, see vv. 11 and 13). The inner certainty of the whole personality is in these verses. The evil man is evil in his total rejection of God.

This total quality of *leb* in many instances, is brought out in the *Shema‘*, from Deuteronomy 6 and quoted by Jesus to the lawyer who would inherit eternal life. 'You shall love the Lord your God with all your heart, and with all your soul, and with all your strength and with all your mind; and your neighbour as yourself' (Luke 10.27; Deut. 6.5; Lev. 19.18). Heart in this passage is one part of a man's make-up but also it may stand for all of a man. A scholar has written, 'Particular passions or emotions will be localized in other internal parts (kidneys, liver), the heart contains them all. It sums up the inward man in opposition to the flesh which is the tangible outward man. A man is worth what his heart is worth' (P. Dhorme, cited by E. Jacob, *Theology of the Old Testament*, p. 166 n.l.).

When we think of giving our hearts to our Lord this word and the pattern of its usage can save us from an emotional, sentimental response alone. In giving our hearts we give our emotions, minds, wills, purposes, that is, ourselves.

> My heart to Thee I give for aye,
> O Jesus, sweetest, best;
> Thy heart to me give Thou, I pray,
> O Jesus, loveliest.

Here is man's total response to God's total gift.

15 · The Servant of the Lord — *'Ebed Yahweh*

It has become unfashionable and almost thought to be a lowering of oneself to be anybody's servant. Yet this is the term that Jesus himself uses to describe his own mission and purpose: 'Among you, whoever wants to be great must be your servant, and whoever wants to be first must be the willing slave of all. For even the Son of Man did not come to be served but to serve and to surrender his life as a ransom for many' (Mark 10.43-45).

Behind this self-chosen role of Servant there is a glorious heritage which we shall briefly sketch. In the Old Testament we see the word translated 'servant'—*'ebed*—used in a number of ways.

The servant is one who tills the ground, the ploughman. In Genesis man is placed in the Garden of Eden to till the ground: 'The Lord God took the man and put him in the garden of Eden to till it and keep it' (Gen. 2.15). The word translated 'till' is from the same stem as that which is later used of the Servant of the Lord. Further, in Ezekiel we read of the ideal age pictured by the prophet: 'Its produce shall be food for the workers of the city. And the workers of the city from all the tribes of Israel shall till it' (Ezek. 48.19). The same root is used for 'workers' and 'till' and it is the root from which '*ebed*—servant—comes. Already we see that the word '*ebed* has a meaning of work, costing and laborious rather than mere status.

The servant and the palace.   From plough to palace, this is the pattern of the usage of the word '*ebed* as we find the word used for serving in the king's court. Thus when the Queen of Sheba visits Solomon and sees the wonder of his household she exclaims: 'Happy are your wives! Happy are these your servants, who continually stand before you and hear your wisdom!' (I Kings 10.8). The servant then may be one who stands before the king or at the plough.

The servant in the Temple.   The word is also used of those who stand before the Lord in the services of the Temple. At the dedication of the Temple, 'When the priests came out of the holy place, a cloud filled the house of the Lord, so that the priests could not stand to minister because of the cloud; for the glory of the Lord filled the house of the lord' (I Kings 8.10-11). Here we see a spiritual pilgrimage from the field of the ploughman to the court of the king, to the altar of the Lord—all are servants. The emphasis is on the activity not the position, the serving not the status.

God's people as his Servant.   The word '*ebed* is used not only of individuals but also of the whole nation. The great prophecies of Deutero-Isaiah reach this climax of thought concerning the role of Israel among the nations of the world. So we read in Isa. 49.6: 'It is too light a thing that you should be my servant to raise up the tribes of Jacob and to restore the preserved of Israel; I will give you as a light to the nations, that my salvation may reach to the end of the earth.' God is saying to the Israelite nation that their future lies not in the status of being his chosen people as if this meant privilege and not responsibility. In fact, they will be his people only if they become servants to the rest of the nations. It is small wonder that many of them rebelled. They just could not stomach the idea of being servants or as it would appear to them, to be subservient door-mats to the rest of the world.

Yet the shock that awaits them after the Exile is even greater. Not only must God's chosen people be servants but they must accept the role of being the Suffering Servant. The picture is drawn in the words of Deutero-Isaiah that are unforgettable: 'He shall see the fruit of the travail of his soul and be satisfied; by his knowledge shall the righteous one, my servant, make many to be accounted righteous; and he shall bear their iniquities ... because he poured out his soul to death, and was numbered with the transgressors; yet he bore the sins of many, and made intercession for the transgressors' (Isa 53.11-12). It is here that Jesus finds the vision of what he is seeking to do as he serves mankind.

The Servant and Suffering. The whole message of the Servant Songs (Isa. 41.1-8; 42.1-9; 49.1-10; 52.13-53.12) is that the Servant must carry out his commission not in spite of his suffering but through the agency and instrumentality of such sorrow. From this source we find the inspiration of the later gospel writings as in Mark 10.43-45: 'But it shall not be so among you; but whoever would be great among you must be your servant, and whoever would be first among you must be slave of all. For the Son of Man also came not to be served but to serve, and to give his life a ransom for many.' The words translated 'servant' and 'serve' are derived from the same root which provides our word 'deacon'. The 'deacon' (A.V. 'minister') is one who ministers and the form of his ministry is that of a servant. So also we have the testimony of Paul: 'Have this mind among yourselves, which you have in Christ Jesus, who, though he was in the form of God, did not count equality with God a thing to be grasped, but emptied himself, taking the form of a servant, being born in the likeness of man. And being found in human form he humbled himself and became obedient unto death, even death on a cross' (Phil. 2.6-9). The word for 'servant' in this passage might equally well be translated 'slave'. It is precisely because of this humbling of himself that exaltation comes. One may serve not in spite of suffering but only through it. Here is the only means by which a man may become a servant. So the thread of the Servant theme runs through the Bible—from plough to palace, from Temple to the Cross, and then to the right hand of God.

> Go, labour on: spend and be spent,
> Thy joy to do the Father's will;
> It is the way the Master went;
> Should not the servant tread it still?

16 · Knowledge of God — da'ath 'Elohim

To know God is the supreme quest for man in every age. When the Bible speaks of knowing God there is always a special emphasis. When we look at the early stories of Genesis we see that there are two questions asked by God that are fundamental for every generation. God asks Adam—Where are you? (Gen. 3.9) and he asks Cain—Where is Abel, your brother? (Gen. 4.9). These questions are about persons not things. They really ask not *what* do you know but *whom*. The Bible when it speaks of knowing means a knowledge that implies a relationship between persons rather than external knowledge of facts. In a sense, this is the difference between science and religion. There is no conflict between the two kinds of knowing yet the Bible insists that the knowledge of a modern technical society must be used to serve the knowledge that we have concerning persons—that is, people count!

The Hebrew word used for 'to know' is *yada'*. A number of scenes will help us to understand the way in which the word is used. In the Fourth Servant Song we read: 'He was despised and

rejected by men; a man of sorrows and acquainted with grief'
(Isa. 53.3). The word translated 'acquainted' is a form of *yada'*
and might be translated, 'He knew within himself the meaning'
of grief. This goes far beyond our phrase—having a nodding
acquaintance with some person. The Suffering Servant knew grief
from inside the experience of it, not as an observer. So in Isa. 47.8
we read of the prophet's judgment upon Babylon: 'Now therefore hear this, you lover of pleasure, who sit securely, who say in
your heart, "I am, and there is no one besides me, I shall not sit
as a widow or know the loss of children."' The boast is in vain
but the meaning is clear that knowing the loss of children is not a
question of information but of involvement in sorrow. (See Gen.
4.2 where knowing is used of the intimate relationship of man
and woman.) From an examination of instances in which the
words 'to know' (*yada'*) or 'knowledge' (*da'ath*) occur the following principles of interpretation emerge.

Knowledge means responsibility rather than privilege. In the
prophecy of Amos we remember a familiar passage: 'Hear this
word that the Lord has spoken against you, O people of Israel,
against the whole family which I have brought up out of the land
of Egypt: you only have I known of all the families of the earth;
therefore I will punish you for all your iniquities' (Amos 3.1-2).
Some of the Israelites must have had the shock of their lives
when they heard these words. We can imagine some of them
saying—Surely, since God has delivered us from the tyranny in
Egypt and known us in a way different from the rest of the world,
we should have special treatment! But the knowledge of God
they had been given meant that they should have known his will
and purpose from the inside of this relationship. Because they
had rejected the opportunity their covenant relationship offered,
they receive special judgment not exemption from it.

Knowledge means personal encounter and communion. A further striking use of the word 'to know'—*yada'*—is found in Psalm
1 where the Two Ways of Life are characterized. The psalm

ends with this couplet: 'For the Lord knows the way of the righteous, but the way of the wicked will perish' (Ps. 1.6). The Lord knows the way of the righteous. This means that they are in fellowship with him. His will and their will are one. Here is a relationship of communion that is the result of God knowing man and man knowing God. Our knowing God must involve a willingness to take the risk of personal encounter. It means daring to know him rather than knowing a number of facts about him. God can never be the object of our knowledge such as some field of study like physics or philosophy. He reveals himself to us and we know him if we are ready for encounter.

Lack of knowledge means rebellion not ignorance.   If knowledge is of the nature of a relationship, then not knowing God is not to be equated with ignorance, not knowing through a lack of information. In Isaiah we read: 'The ox knows its owner, and the ass its master's crib; but Israel does not know, my people does not understand' (Isa. 1.3). The prophet sees that to be without the knowledge of God means rebellion, the refusal of a relationship. So Hosea describes God's controversy with Israel: 'My people enquire of a thing of wood and their staff gives them oracles. For a spirit of harlotry has led them astray, and they have left their God to play the harlot' (Hos. 4.12). The word used for 'to play the harlot' is *zanah*—to act as a prostitute. This involves the breaking of the relationship. It is not a mistake, it is a sin.

Knowledge involves action as well as observation.   A recent comment concerning our knowledge of God has been: 'The intimate response of men's whole being to God is what the Bible means by knowledge of God.' To know the truth about God leads us to carry out his will and purpose. It is in the light of these passages from the Old Testament that we must interpret the passage in John 3.21: 'But he who does what is true comes to the light, that it may be clearly seen that his deeds have been wrought in God.' We leave the balcony for the arena once we come to the knowledge of God. Even more than this, the decision to act is it-self the means of confirming the knowledge. 'If any man's will is to do his will he shall know whether the teaching is from God or whether I am speaking on my own authority' (John 7.17). The knowledge of God brings in 'the bottom of my heart as well as the top of my mind'.

17 · Man and his Sin — *chatta'th, 'avon, pesha'*

The great fact behind the Bible story is that God is with his people. He has chosen them and he is in fellowship with them—this is the presupposition of some of the words we have examined such as holiness and righteousness. What of the other side of the relationship between God and man? How does man react to God's action? The answer is short and straight—he sins! He puts him-self against God. The Old Testament does not use one single word to describe man's alienation from God but rather a number of terms to express this universal experience. The main terms are *chatta'th 'avon* and *pesha'*.

Sin as missing the mark. The most usual word used for men's wrongdoing is *chatta'th*, which is used of missing a mark or target set. We find an illustration of this in Judg. 20.16 where in the mustering of the forces from the tribe of Benjamin we find the description, 'Among all these were seven hundred picked men who were left-handed; every one could sling a stone at a hair, and not miss.' The significant fact for us is that the words translated 'not miss' are later used of committing sin against man and God. The word used has the same root *chatta'*. In Prov. 19.2 the same word is used: 'It is not good for a man to be without knowledge, and he who makes haste with his feet misses his way.' Again in Job 5.24 Eliphaz speaks to Job of the blessings that will come to him if he turns to God, 'You shall know that your tent is safe and you shall inspect your fold and miss nothing.' We see in these examples the basic idea of falling short of a target or a standard.

So again when Abraham tries to pass off his wife Sarah as his sister, he is challenged by Abimelech, 'What have you done to us? And how have I sinned against you that you have brought on me and my kingdom a great sin? You have done to me things that ought not to be done' (Gen. 20.9). The word for 'sinned' is a form of *chatta'* and clearly the sin belongs to the things that ought not to be done. A standard has not been reached.

Sin as a perversion, a twisting. A second term used for sin in the Old Testament is *'avon* and it is used with a sense of twisting from an original straightness, a perversion. Some examples will bring this meaning out. In Jer. 3.21 we read of the prophet's pleading with Israel to return to her former allegiance to God: 'A voice on the bare heights is heard, the weeping and pleading of Israel's sons, because they have perverted their way, they have forgotten the Lord their God.' The essential note is that the former relationship with God has been twisted and distorted from the original straight way. So Elihu advises Job to accept his suffering from God as a chastening and describes the consequences if he were to do this: 'Then man prays to God, and he accepts him, he comes into his presence with joy. He recounts to man his salvation, and he sings before men, and says: "I have sinned, and perverted what was right, and it was not requited to me"' (Job 33.26-27). Here is a second strand in the Old Testament picture of men pitting themselves against God—the twisting and perverting of the powers that God has given them. When we sin we twist and pervert an original purpose as well as miss the mark.

Sin as personal rebellion. The most significant and profound term used for sin in the Old Testament is *pesha'*. We find it used especially where the central idea is that of a person who rebels against another and wilfully breaks up a relationship. It is used of a son rebelling against his father (Isa. 1.2), of Israel breaking away from the House of David (I Kings 12.19) and of rebellion against the law of God (Hos. 8.1). In particular two passages are of the greatest significance for understanding this act of rebellion.

In one of the moving penitential psalms we hear the cry, 'For I know my transgressions, and my sin is ever before me. Against thee, thee only, have I sinned, and done that which is evil in thy sight' (Ps. 51.3-4). Sin, at its deepest is always 'against thee, thee only'. We are reminded of the cry of the prodigal (Luke 15.18) and supremely the plea from Gethsemane : 'Yet not what I will, but what thou wilt' (Mark 14.36). Knowing no personal rebellion he knew no sin.

In the use of these various words, *chatta'th, 'avon, pesha'*, we find abiding insights into the nature of sin. Lest we think too lightly shall we ask, what targets have we missed, what qualities have we perverted and twisted and where and against whom have we rebelled? We, as men against God, must learn that our only security is in Christ.

In words of John Donne we find the only answer to Everyman who has found himself against God.

> Wilt thou forgive that sinn, by which I'have wonne
> Others to sinn, and made my sinn their dore?
> Wilt thou forgive that sinn which I did shunne
> A yeare or twoe, but wallowed in a score?
> When thou hast done, thou hast not done,
> For I have more.

> I have a sinn of feare that when I have spunn
> My last thred, I shall perish on the shore;
> Sware by thy self that at my Death, thy Sonne
> Shall shine as he shines nowe, and heretofore;
> And having done that, thou hast done,
> I feare noe more.

18 · God's Atonement — *kaphar, kapporeth*

The climax of the Hebrew religious year was the Day of Atonement. On this day the High Priest gathers up the sins of the whole nation and through the rite of the scapegoat, the whole community are rid of the burden of guilt. We find the scene described in Leviticus 16: 'And Aaron shall lay both his hands upon the head of the live goat, and confess over him all the iniquities of the people of Israel, and all their transgressions, all their sins; and he shall put them upon the head of the goat, and send him away into the wilderness by the hand of a man who is in readiness. The goat shall bear all their iniquities upon him to a solitary land; and he shall let the goat go into the wilderness' (vv. 21-22).

Behind this solemn act there is one purpose—that the people might be brought again into a worthy relationship with God, their sins forgiven. The sins must be removed and in this symbolic action it is God himself who brings about the atonement since the goat must be brought before him. It is God who brings about the transfer of the sins. The key word we must consider is the one translated 'atonement' in the earlier part of the chapter (vv. 6, 10). The root is *kaphar* and we find it also in the form *kapporeth* —translated 'mercy-seat' in such a passage as 'And you shall put into the ark the testimony which I shall give you. Then you shall make a mercy seat of pure gold' (Ex. 25.16-17). We shall gain a greater insight into what atonement meant as we consider the ways in which the word *kaphar* is used.

Atonement as a wiping-off.   In the account of the building of the Ark in Gen. 6.14 we find the word *kaphar* used with a meaning of smoothing or spreading. In this instance, it is used of covering the ark with pitch. The physical action is the same, a wiping or spreading whether on or off. In Isaiah's Call Vision we read: 'And he touched my mouth and said: Behold this has touched your lips; and your guilt is taken away, and your sins forgiven' (Isa. 6.7). The same word *kaphar* is used for 'forgiven'. It is used again by Jeremiah as he complains to God of the religious leaders of the nation who plot against him. He cannot bear this without protest and cries out, 'Yet, thou, O Lord, knowest their plotting to slay me. Forgive not their iniquity, nor blot out their sin from thy sight' (Jer. 18.23). In these instances the physical action of wiping deepens in meaning to represent the forgiveness of God who acts as if the wiped out sin is no longer there. We need to be sure that this is no easy wiping the slate clean but the costly grace of God's love that he alone can give. It is God alone who wipes out the sin through grace, not man who wipes out in order to deceive God.

Atonement as a covering-over. Another usage of *kaphar* is in the sense of covering over and so hide from sight as if not there. God in his grace is thought of as covering over the sin of man. The initiative must again be God's alone. No man could so cover over sin that God would not know. It is God's covering over that we find in such passages as the Song of Moses where the sins of the land are covered over, atoned for: 'Praise his people, O you nations; for he avenges the blood of his servants, and takes vengeance upon his adversaries, and makes expiation for the land of his people' (Deut. 32.43). The translation 'makes expiation' is a rendering of *kaphar*—to cover over. So a person's guilt is covered over in Deut. 21.8 where the crime of murder has been committed by an unknown person: 'Forgive, O Lord, thy people Israel, whom thou hast redeemed, and set not the guilt of innocent blood in the midst of thy people Israel; but let the guilt of blood be forgiven them.'

Atonement as a renewal of relationship with God. In a number of passages we see that the end purpose of the atonement is that through forgiveness given and received a reconciliation is effected. The former relationship between God and man may be resumed because this is what God wants, not that man has earned or qualified for atonement. This forgiving, reconciling action of God is seen in two further passages where *kaphar* is used. The psalmist cries, 'O thou who hearest prayer! To thee shall all flesh come on account of sins. When our transgressions prevail over us, thou dost forgive them' (Ps. 65.2-3). Again the wisdom writer affirms, 'By loyalty and faithfulness iniquity is atoned for, and by the fear of the Lord a man avoids evils' (Prov. 16.6). The 'fear of the Lord' in this last passage stands for the relationship with

God a man may have through the acceptance of forgiveness. The atoning can only be accepted from within not from outside the 'fear of the Lord'.

Atonement for his own sake.   As we see the development of the idea of atonement we leave behind the angry God who has to be placated through human ritual or even magical action. We see that God forgives, atones, as an expression of what he is like. God initiates the conditions under which he and man may start again in a covenant relationship. So the prophet Deutero-Isaiah records the voice of God speaking, 'I, I am he who blots out your transgressions for my own sake, I will not remember your sins' (Isa. 43.25). This is not the last word that God speaks but he, through Christ, fulfils the words of the same prophet. 'But he was wounded for our transgressions, he was bruised for our iniquities; upon him was the chastisement that made us whole, and with his stripes we are healed' (Isa. 53.5).

19 · **The Search for Wisdom** — *chokmah*

Where can Wisdom be found? This is the search of Everyman. It is the quest of the philosopher as the very name suggests—lover of wisdom—and it is the goal of all men's seeking in the unfolding story of the Bible. We shall see the wealth of the biblical concept of wisdom as we glance at the various ways in which the word *chokmah* is used in the Old Testament.

Wisdom as technical skill.   In a number of passages the word is used to describe what we today would call technical efficiency in such fields as military prowess (Isa. 10.13); in the skills of the goldsmith and other artisans (Jer. 10.9); and the skill of women in spinning and weaving the furnishings of the Temple (Ex. 28.3; 31.6; 35.25). In these passages the wise man and the wise woman is the skilled person who knows how to do the job. Wisdom may be equated with the 'know-how'.

Wisdom as the ultimate goal.   As well as the practical wisdom of knowing how to deal with the practical, immediate situations of everyday life there is a level of thought in which *chokmah* is used to describe the ultimate secrets of God's dealing with his world. Thus Job speaks: 'But where shall wisdom be found? And where is the place of understanding? Man does not know the way to it, and it is not found in the land of the living. The deep says, "It is not in me," and the sea says, "It is not in me." It cannot be gotten for gold, and silver cannot be weighed as its price. . . .' He continues, 'God understands the way to it, and he knows its place' (Job 28.12-15, 23). Beyond the level of the proverbial wisdom of everyday experience that has crystallized over the years (see Proverbs 15 throughout), here is a wisdom that man cannot gain by search however thorough. No religious technique can guarantee success in this quest for the wisdom that is in the possession of God and, as his grace, he can give to whom he pleases. This element of *givenness* in wisdom is seen at the close of the Hymn to Wisdom from which we quoted in Job 28. He concludes, 'And he said to man, "Behold, the fear of the Lord, that is wisdom; and to depart from evil is understanding" ' (v. 28). By the phrase, 'the fear of the Lord', the Bible means all that we today mean by religion. The whole range of man's relationship to God is in this phrase. Wisdom becomes no cloistered virtue but the gift of God to men who are committed and dedicated to his purpose.

Wisdom as person. We have seen the advance from wisdom as a practical skill to wisdom as the supreme gift of God given in covenant relationship with those who fear him. The Bible takes us further and we find wisdom at least personified and many would say, thought of as an extension of the personality of God. We see this especially in Prov. 8.22-27: 'The Lord created me at the beginning of his work, the first of his acts of old. Ages ago I was set up at the first, before the beginning of the earth. When there were no depths I was brought forth. . . . When he established the heavens, I was there . . . then I was beside him, like a master workman' (vv. 22-24, 27, 30).

Wisdom and Spirit.   In two passages from the apocryphal literature where the Hebrew idea of wisdom is developed even more fully we find an identification between Wisdom and Spirit. These are found in the Wisdom of Solomon and read: 'For Wisdom is a kindly spirit and will not free a blasphemer from the guilt of his words: because God is a witness of his inmost feelings, and a true observer of his heart, and a hearer of his tongue. Because the Spirit of the Lord has filled the world, and that which holds all things together knows what is said' (1.6-7). The second passage is: 'For wisdom, the fashioner of all things taught me. For in her there is a spirit that is intelligent, holy, unique, manifold. . . . For she is a breath of the power of God, and a pure emanation of the glory of the Almighty . . .' (7.22f).

Here Wisdom and Spirit are identified.

Christ as the Wisdom of God.   The Hebrew concept of *chokmah* —wisdom—reaches its climax beyond even the aprocryphal writings, in the New Testament. Here we find that Christ is called the Wisdom of God. In the Gospels we read: 'Therefore also the Wisdom of God said, "I will send them prophets and apostles, some of whom they will kill and persecute" ' (Luke 11.49 and see Matt. 23.34-36). Again Paul speaks: 'For Jews demand signs and Greeks seek wisdom, but we preach Christ crucified, a stumbling block to Jews and folly to the Gentiles, but to those who are called, both Jews and Greeks, Christ the power of God and the wisdom of God' (I Cor. 1.22-24; see also I Cor. 2.6 f.; 1.16-17). In these passages we see the self-identification of Christ as the Wisdom of God; and Paul as he seeks to express all that Christ meant to him sees a Wisdom of God that destroys the wisdom of the wise (I Cor. 1.19). The wisdom of the mind alone, of technical skill or intellectual arrogance divorced from the personal relationship of man with God—this wisdom God has made folly.

The biblical concept of Wisdom carries its own challenge. Have we thought that salvation by knowledge is possible? Is there a

remaining belief in redemption by technics? We need to hear
Wisdom speak as of old when she invited all to come to the table
set: 'Come, eat of my bread and drink of the wine I have mixed'
(Prov. 9.5). We know now that we may drink and eat at a richer
table since Christ, the supreme gift of God, is the Wisdom of God
given to all who come.

20 · **Return!** — *shub*

Whatever you say you can't change human nature! So many
have repeated this verdict in every generation since Jeremiah
posed his question, 'Can the Ethiopian change his skin or the
leopard his spots?' (Jer. 13.15). The context of the question is
that of a man desperately concerned about his own nation who
have rejected the word of God. The situation is dramatically
drawn in Jer. 5.1: 'Run to and fro through the streets of Jerusalem
look and take note! Search her squares to see if you can find a
man, one who does justice and seeks truth, that I may pardon her.'
The city is in an even worse plight than Sodom of old. When
Abraham intercedes with God for that evil community he receives the reply, 'For the sake of ten I will not destroy it' (Gen.
18.23-32).

Return—the only way forward. The prophet knows only one
way of meeting his people's rebellion. They must return to God.
Return! The word used is *shub* and it is found as a refrain recurring again and again in the Old Testament and especially in
Jeremiah. Thus we read in Deuteronomy 30 of the crucial choice
put before the people: 'And when all these things come upon you,
the blessing and the curse, which I have set before you, and you
call them to mind among all the nations where the Lord has driven
you, and return to the Lord your God, you and your children,
and obey his voice in all that I command you this day, with all
your heart and with all your soul' (vv. 1-3 and also Deut. 4.25-
31).

In Jeremiah we have six occurrences of the theme—return—

in Chapter 3 alone: 'Return, faithless Israel, says the Lord. I will not look on you in anger, for I am merciful, says the Lord; I will not be angry for ever' (v. 12, see also vv. 1, 7, 9, 14, 22 and 4.1).

Returning means an inner revolution. The summons to the prophet to return means that the whole will must be surrendered to a new purpose and cause. The prophets knew that the malady of Israel was deep-seated, and Hosea, a contemporary of Jeremiah, cries out: 'What shall I do with you, O Ephraim? What shall I do with you, O Judah? Your love is like a morning cloud, like the dew that goes away early' (Hos. 6.4). No change in a cultic technique or a sacrificial rite will answer the need of his people: 'The heart is deceitful above all things, and desperately wicked, corrupt, who can understand it?' (Jer. 17.10). No external change but an inner revolution. This is the burden of the great concept of the Inner Covenant: 'I will put my law within them, and I will write it upon their hearts and I will be their God, and they shall be my people' (Jer. 31.31-34). A further characteristic of the way in which *shub* is used in the fact that only in one instance (Isa. 30.15) is the noun—*shubah* (returning)—used in the whole Old Testament. This is underlined by Jacob, who writes, 'Conversion can never be considered as a quality that man could possess as his own; in the Old Testament there are no converted men but only beings who are incessantly converted' (E. Jacob, *Theology of the Old Testament*, p. 289 n.2). A man must return to God in his innermost thought and being—and he must do so again and again.

Only God can initiate the turning of man. The problem for man still remains. How can he obtain the power to so re-orientate his life towards God? Both prophet and psalmist realize that the deepest truth of their plight is that they are dependent upon God for their very turning back to him. Only God can supply the initiative and dynamic. So God speaks to Jeremiah about his people: 'I have heard Ephraim bemoaning, "Thou hast chastened me, and I was chastened, like an untrained calf; bring me back that I may be restored, for thou art the Lord, my God" ' (Jer. 31.18). The same insight is shown by the psalmist in Psalm 80 where the following refrain is repeated three times: 'Make us return, O God; let thy face shine, that we may be saved' (vv. 3, 7, 19). The R.S.V. reads 'restore' but the original form is *shub* in the causative form—*hashibenu*—cause us to return! Return we must, yet God alone can bring us round in our tracks to return to him.

Return and recommission. A final note needs to be sounded especially for the servants of God, commissioned to call people to return to God. What of the prophet himself? There is no exemption. He himself, spokesman of God, must be converted anew. He must return to receive his commission anew. His knowledge of God's dealings must be of utter grace. 'Therefore thus says the Lord: "If you return, I will restore you and you shall stand before me. If you utter what is precious, and not what is worthless, you shall be as my mouth" ' (Jer. 15.19). In returning alone lies our safety. This returning must be initiated by God, it must change our inner lives and it is a presupposition of bidding others return. So Francis Thompson has described the step that we all must take:

> All which I took from thee I did but take,
> not for thy harms,
> But just that thou might'st seek it in My arms.
> All which thy child's mistake
> Fancies as lost, I have restored for thee at home:
> Rise, clasp My hand, and come!

21 · A Man's Hope — *qavah*

Waiting upon the Lord! To earlier generations the phrase 'wait upon the Lord' had deep undertones of fellowship and communion with God. It was used to express the intimacy of a man's prayer life and meditation. We remember the haunting use of the phrase in Deutero-Isaiah, 'Even youths shall faint and be weary, and young men shall fall exhausted; but they who wait for the Lord shall renew their strength, they shall mount up with wings like eagles, they shall run and not be weary, they shall walk and not faint' (Isa. 40.30-31).

The word translated 'wait' in the passage quoted is *qavah* and we find it used in a number of contexts that together give some idea of the riches that lie behind the expression 'waiting on the Lord'.

The scarlet thread of Rahab.   The probable basic meaning of *qavah* is 'to twist as a thread' and this meaning is brought out in the dramatic story of Rahab and her hiding of the spies. So we read in Josh. 2.18 and 21: 'Behold when we come into the land, you shall bind this scarlet cord in the window through which you let us down. . . . Then she sent them away, and they departed; and she bound the scarlet cord in the window.' The word rendered 'cord' comes from the same root as the word translated 'wait for' in Isaiah 40.

Waiting in ambush.   A second picture of a different context is found in the Psalter. There are two passages where the scene is laid for an ambush and the word used to convey this expectancy and urgency is *qavah*. In Psalm 56 we read of the psalmist's complaint against his enemies who oppress him: 'They shall gather themselves together, they hide themselves, they mark my steps, when they wait for my soul' (v. 7). Further in Psalm 119 we have: 'I will never forget thy precepts; for by them thou hast given me life. I am thine, save me. For I have sought thy precepts. The wicked lie in wait to destroy me; but I consider thy testimonies' (vv. 93-5). The waiting in these verses is that of the evildoers in ambush for their victims. Yet the expectancy, the sense of being eager and tensed ready for action is a challenge that is inescapable. Although the hoping is allied to an evil purpose, the tension and urgency is there.

God's waiting upon man.   The word *qavah* is also used of God and his waiting upon man. We find this changed relationship in the Song of the Vineyard in Isaiah 5. This is a parable of God's expectation that after all he has done for his people they will turn from their evil ways. God pleads poignantly: 'What more was there to do for my vineyard, that I have not done in it? When I looked for it to yield grapes, why did it yield wild grapes? (v. 4) . . . For the vineyard of the Lord of Hosts is the house of Israel, and the men of Judah are his pleasant planting; and he looked for justice, but behold, a cry!' (v. 7).

The word translated 'looked for' is *qavah* and is used in the expression 'Wait on the Lord'. God waits in his expectancy, he has hope of his people but it is dashed to the ground. In the fuller light of the revelation in Christ, we know that even if the son of the master of the vineyard is killed yet he still stands at the door and knocks waiting in hope to enter. He is waiting and hoping for man's response (see Matt. 21.33 and Rev. 3.20).

Waiting and renewal.   Our final picture is that from which our opening phrase was taken. It is that of refugees in a strange land, facing the ardours of the long trek back to the homeland, the risks of the journey and the long drawn-out period of re-adjustment as they seek to settle again in the land God had given to their fathers. It is this minority group of returning exiles that are the first hearers of the prophet's words: 'He gives power to the faint, and to him who has no might he increases strength. Even youths shall faint and be weary, and young men shall fall exhausted; but they who wait for the Lord shall renew their strength, they shall mount up with wings as eagles, they shall run and not be weary, they shall walk and not faint' (Isa. 40.30-31).

The actual Hebrew for 'renew' is a word that means to change. It is not so much an increase of a man's resources but a change to a new source of power—the strength of God given to those who 'wait for' the Lord.

The series of pictures behind the use of *qavah*—the tension of the cord, the waiting in ambush, the pleading of God and the new source of power for homesick refugees all are part of the richness of the word. All these strands are fittingly summed up by the psalmist when he affirms: 'For thou, O Lord art my hope (*qavah*), my trust, O Lord from my youth' (Ps. 71.5). God is himself a man's hope, the one upon whom he waits and depends as his life-line.

22 · The Day of the Lord —*Yom Yahweh*

The great characteristic of the Old Testament is that the writers are convinced that the best is yet to be! There is, of course, a look backward to what the Lord has done for his people seen especially in the constant references to the deliverance from Egypt at the Exodus. This became an integral part of the early *credos* so that we find in such passages as Deut. 6.20-25:

'We were Pharaoh's slaves in Egypt; and the Lord brought us out of Egypt with a mighty hand; and the Lord showed signs and wonders, great and grievous, against Egypt and against Pharaoh and all his household, before our eyes; and he brought us out from there, that he might bring us in and give us the land which he swore to give to our fathers.' (See also Josh. 24.1-8.)

Yet the Israelites look back in order to look forward with all the more certainty to the time when God would again defeat all the enemies of Israel and exalt his chosen people; this dream of the future is crystallized in the term 'the Day of the Lord'—*Yom Yahweh*.

The original meaning of Yom Yahweh. A valuable suggestion concerning the original meaning of 'The Day of the Lord' has been put forward by W. Robertson Smith in his book, *The Prophets of Israel* (2nd ed. [1928], p. 398). He cites a number of Arabic parallels which indicate that the full connotation of 'day' is 'the day of battle' and affirms that 'By taking the day of Yahweh to mean His day of battle and victory we gain for the conception a natural basis in Hebrew idiom.' Some passages that support this view are Isa. 9.4 and Judg. 7.9. The first reads, 'For the yoke of his burden, and the staff of his shoulder, the rod of his oppressor, thou hast broken as in the day of Midian.' The reference to the day of Midian is made clear when we read in Judg. 7.9: 'That same night the Lord said to him (Gideon), "Arise go down against the camp; for I have given it into your hand." ' The 'day of Midian' stands certainly for a day when victory over Midian was gained through the power and might of God. His day is his day of victorious battle.

The Day of the Lord and the man in the street. We find that the term 'the Day of the Lord' is expressed in a number of passages revealing the dominant features associated with it in the mind of the people.

So in Amos 5.18-20 we read, 'Woe to you who desire the day of the Lord! Why would you have the day of the Lord? It is darkness, and not light! As if a man fled from a lion, and a bear met him; or went into the house and leaned with his hand against the wall, and a serpent bit him. Is not the day of the Lord darkness, and not light, and gloom with no brightness in it?' Or in Zeph. 3.9: 'Therefore wait for me, says the Lord. For the day when I arise as a witness. For my decision is to gather nations, to assemble kingdoms, to pour out upon them my indignation, all the heat of my anger: for in the fire of my jealous wrath all the earth shall be consumed.' In Isaiah too the idea appears: 'Wail, for the day of the Lord is near; as destruction from the Almighty it will come!' (Isa. 13.6). The prophet Ezekiel echoes the same note: 'Son of man, prophesy and say, Thus says the Lord God: Wail, "Alas for the day! For the day is near, the day of the Lord is near; it will be a day of clouds, a time of doom for the nations" ' (Ezek. 30.2-3). These four passages from the prophets underline the main characteristic features of the Day of the Lord. They can be summarized: judgment, universality, involving a supernatural intervention, and to many—a day that is imminent!

Day of the Lord and moral judgment. From the oldest passage that contains the phrase, Amos 5.18-20 we have seen that the idea of such a day is familiar in the eighth century B.C. The only question is what sort of day would it really be? The very insistence of Amos especially but supported by the other prophets (see Hos. 5.9; Isa. 2.17; Micah 2.4; Zeph. 1.7, 8) upon the fact that it will be a day of judgment suggests that this is a reversal of popular expectation. The current belief attacked by the prophets is that the day was one when Israel would be vindicated against all her enemies just because she is Israel, the chosen people. The burden of the use made by Amos is that Israel would also be judged on that day! What he does is to bring a dimension of moral depth to the term—the Day of the Lord will be the Day when his moral will and purpose will be vindicated among all the nations of the earth, without any special favoured nation clause!

The Day of the Lord and the golden age. A final association of the Day of the Lord (*Yom Yahweh*) is its link with Israel's Golden Age. Although men could strive to carry out God's purpose and accept the will of the Lord for his people as their destiny, the Golden Age could neither be engineered or manipulated into existence. The Golden Age must be God's gift—it is always his Day. This is implicit in a number of passages that look forward to a glorious future whether the actual term is used or not. So the picture is painted, never in merely political or economic terms but having a spiritual foundation. Three prophets picture for us the Day of the Lord that is to come. First, in Isa. 2.4: 'It shall come to pass in the latter days that the mountain of the Lord shall be established as the highest of the mountains and shall be raised above the hills; and all nations shall flow to it, and many peoples shall come and say: "Come, let us go up to the mountain of the Lord, to the house of the God of Jacob; that he may teach us his ways and that we may walk in his paths." For out of Zion shall go forth the law, and the word from Jerusalem. He shall judge between nations and shall decide for many peoples; and they shall beat their swords into plowshares, and their spears into pruning hooks; nation shall not lift up sword against nation, neither shall they learn war any more.' Again in Zech. 2.11 we read: 'And many nations shall join themselves to the Lord in that day, and shall be my people; and I will dwell in the midst of you.' Here we have the note of the Covenant (see Jer. 31.34) but extended beyond the barriers of the Hebrew nation—all the walls are down in the Golden Age—the Day of the Lord is for all people.

III

CONCERNING THE COMMUNITY
AND THE CULT

ONE of the characteristics of Israelite thought is that though there existed the structure of the state, involving for a time the monarchy and civil institutions, in reality the nation remained a religious community and all its institutions were judged by the religious faith of a people in covenant relationship with God.

We may draw no hard and fast line between cult and community since religious impulses and motives permeated the whole life of Hebrew society. The term cult is used to describe the actions and institutions that this community used, to give expression to its sense of relationship with God, that is, to respond to the Creator.

The Hebrew cult is to be distinguished from the cultic pattern of the Ancient Near East, whatever the external similarities even of ritual action, by the following affirmations of Israel's faith.

God is the only God and there is no other.
God is a Person in covenant relation with persons and not the embodiment of a force or process of nature.
God is so transcendant that no image could be adequate.
God is Spirit.[1]

23 · **Blood** — *dam, damim*

The word used for blood in the Old Testament is *dam* or *damim* and from the earliest accounts we see that a mystery surrounds the thought of blood for every nation. The two poles of life—

[1] See R. de Vaux, *Ancient Israel, Its Life and Institutions*, 1962, pp. 271–3.

birth and death—would be related to the issue of blood in childbirth or the death resulting from a loss of blood. These crucial experiences with their associations form part of the awe with which blood is thought of, especially in a world without the knowledge which we have today. The essentials of biblical thought concerning this fundamental reality may be summarized under four heads.

Blood and God's prerogative. From the vital quality of blood (*dam, damim*) and the certainty that God alone is the Lord of life, it follows that he is the only one who may dispose of it when devoted to him. This results in a series of prohibitions relating to blood. Two are of especial significance. Men are forbidden to eat meat with the blood still in it. So in Deut. 12.23 we read: 'Only be sure that you do not eat the blood; for the blood is the life, and you shall not eat the life with the flesh' (see also Gen. 9.4; Lev. 17.10-11). The emphasis is theological rather than hygienic. God is the sovereign lord of life, so that no man may seek to increase his life-power by eating the blood of an animal thus bypassing God's authority over life and death. Similarly, we find an edict against the shedding of blood. This is not primarily a recognition that murder is anti-social but a realization that the right of God must not be spurned and put aside. So we read in Genesis 9: 'Only you shall not eat flesh with its life, that is, its blood. For your lifeblood I will surely require a reckoning; of every beast I will require it and of man; of every man's brother I will require the life of man. Whoever sheds the blood of man, by man shall his blood be shed; for God made man in his own image' (vv. 4-6).

Blood represents life more than death. A central passage will illustrate this emphasis: 'For the life of the flesh is in the blood; and I have given it for you upon the altar to make atonement for your souls; for it is the blood that makes atonement, by reason of the life' (Lev. 17.11). The great value behind the Hebrew sacrificial practice is not so much the act of offering what is valuable to God through the killing of an animal but that through this act the life is released and given to God. Sacrifice is better seen as a release of life than just a shedding of blood. The Day of Atonement was for the Hebrew nation a new beginning not an ending and this was brought about through the life that was in the blood (see Lev. 16 and 17). When later generations think of Calvary, the same note must be sounded —that the shedding of Christ's blood means life rather than death.

Blood stands for the power to protect.   A further feature of the meaning of blood in the Old Testament is that it was believed to have the power to protect. The well-known story of the Passover rite will illustrate this. In the tension between Pharaoh and Moses, this is the crowning test of strength. The Angel of Death will smite the firstborn of the Egyptians. The safeguard for the Israelites and their families lies in the smearing of blood on the doorposts and lintel of their houses. Blood protects and saves. Thus we read in Exodus 12: 'For the Lord will pass through to slay the Egyptians; and when he sees the blood on the lintel and on the two doorposts, the Lord will pass over the door, and will not allow the destroyer to enter the houses to slay you' (v. 23). To our minds that may seem somewhat naïve, even magical. Yet we must translate into the thought of our day this essential principle that there is safety and protection in the self-giving of Christ's blood.

Blood is a medium of communion.   A final strand in this biblical pattern relates to communion between God and man. Two passages spring to mind. The scene of the first is that of an eager, expectant congregation. Moses, the representative of God and man, is on the point of carrying out the sacrificial act that will bring God and man together; the oxen have been killed and the drained blood is thrown, half upon the altar and half over the congregation. This was a sacred act and through the life of the third party—the ox—God and man are united in sharing a common life (see Ex. 24.6-8). Over the centuries we come next to the Upper Room and Jesus our High Priest (see Heb. 2.17) takes the cup and says: 'This cup is the new covenant in my blood' (I Cor. 11.25).

The modes of bringing God and man into communion may differ but the common symbol is the blood. How can I approach God on my own? What can I take as an offering? The greatest offering we can make is Christ's self-offering of his blood. Here is our guarantee of life, salvation and communion.

> Just as I am, without one plea
> But that Thou bid'st me come to Thee,
> O Lamb of God, I come.

24 · The Lord's Passover — *pesach Yahweh*

The religious experience of the Hebrews reached its peak in the great festivals, namely, the Feast of Unleavened Bread, the Feast of Weeks at the time of the wheat harvest and the Feast of Ingathering. These are the great cultic occasions when every male was expected to appear before Yahweh three times a year (Ex. 34.23).

The festivals and history. The very names of these festivals indicate an agricultural origin. We note the absence of any reference to the Passover, yet this is the theme of our present study— *Pesach Yahweh*—the Lord's Passover. In the same way as the Christian Church later has used pagan festivals in the celebration of the Birth and Resurrection of Jesus Christ at Christmas and Easter so these feasts became linked up in the Hebrew mind with the great acts of deliverance that God their Saviour had wrought especially in the experiences of the Exodus from Egypt. Thus, at a later date the Feast of Weeks (Pentecost) was associated with the giving of the Law of God to Moses on Sinai and the Feast of Ingathering with the Wandering in the Wilderness (Lev. 23.42f.):

'You shall dwell in booths for seven days; all that are native in Israel shall dwell in booths, that your generation may know that I made the people of Israel dwell in booths when I brought them out of the land of Egypt: I am the Lord your God.'

Especially we are concerned with the Passover or *pesach* festival. So we read the account of its significance in Ex. 34.18: 'The Feast of unleavened bread you shall keep. Seven days you shall eat unleavened bread, as I commanded you at the time appointed in the month Abib; for in the month Abib you came out of Egypt.' The actual meaning of the eating of unleavened bread is seen in the normal practice of eating from new grain in the native religious practice before the time of Moses in Canaan. It would be eaten when ready rather than at a set date. What has happened is that the natural cycle of nature worship is adapted as a vehicle to bear witness not to a process but to the personal God Yahweh who has intervened in history to save his people. Here is the emphasis not on Nature but on Nature's God. The Passover reaches its fullest interpretation in the Person of Christ as we shall see later. Our emphasis now is that these festivals and particularly the Passover are seen as occasions when God's personal intervention in human history is celebrated.

The meaning of Pesach—*Passover.* The term that is used for this festival—*pesach Yahweh* (the Lord's Passover)—is used with the sense of 'to limp'. We find this meaning in the account of Elijah's conflict with the priests of Baal at Mount Carmel in I Kings 18.21 and 26. Elijah deliberately plays upon the word when he taunts them: 'How long will you go limping between two different opinions?' The word for 'limping' is a form of the same stem from which *pesach* comes and the reference is to the unsteady gait of a lame man. The verse is a contemptuous comment on a part of the ritual connected with Baal worship which apparently included some form of dance. So we read again, 'And they took the bull which was given them and they prepared it and called upon the name of Baal from morning until noon, saying, O Baal, answer us! But there was no voice, and no one answered. And they limped about the altar which they had made.'

From the sense of being lame or limping the usage changed to include the sense of limping over so to spare or pass over. This provides the obvious link with the account of the institution of the Passover we find in Ex. 12.13: 'The blood shall be a sign for you, upon the houses where you are; and when I see the blood, I will pass over you (*pesach*) and no plague shall fall upon you to destroy you, when I smite the land of Egypt.' (See also vv. 23, 27.)

The Passover and the present generation. The characteristic features of the passover were five-fold: i. the sacrifice of an animal from the flock or herd, ii. the smearing of blood at the tent entrance, iii. the eating of the communal meal, iv. a form of ritual dance, and v. its association with the period of the full moon. Originally a nomadic moon festival designed to ward off evil spirits and to increase fertility of the flock, it became the means whereby the true Israelites in every generation identified themselves with God's saving act in delivering his people from Egypt. There is a prescribed answer for the head of the household whenever he is questioned by the young of succeeding generations: 'What do you mean by this service?' He must reply, 'It is the sacrifice of the Lord's Passover (*pesach*), for he passed over the houses of the people of Israel in Egypt; when he slew the Egyptian but spared (*pesach*) our houses' (Ex. 12.26-27). The emphasis is upon the act of remembering what God has done and is still able and willing to do. The celebration of the Passover is a *re-presenting* of the Exodus as a present event in which the devout of every generation know themselves to be taking part. The Hebrew word for 'to remember' (*zakar*) has this sense of re-enacting here and now events of the past. To this day the following words are used by the devout Jew.

In every generation it is a man's duty to regard himself as if he had come forth from Egypt as Scripture tells. 'And you shall tell your son on that day, "It is because of what the Lord did *for me* when *I* came out of Egypt"' (Ex. 13.8). It was not our fathers alone that the Holy One, blessed be he, redeemed; but *us as well did he redeem* together with them, as Scripture tells: 'And he brought *us* out from there, that he might bring *us* in and give *us* the land which he sware to give to our fathers' (Deut. 6.23).

We see readily that it is precisely in the same frame of mind and spirit that we approach the great acts of God performed through Christ on Calvary.

Christ our Passover.   Supremely we find this theme of *re-presenting* the deliverance that God has wrought for his people in the direct link between the Passover and Christ. Whether or not the Last Supper was the actual Passover meal or a fellowship meal preparatory to the festival, this much is certain that all the associations of the Passover would be present when Jesus says, 'This is my body which is for you' and 'This cup is the new covenant in my blood. Do this as oft as you drink it, in remembrance of me' (I Cor. 11.23-26). Ever since that night, when his followers have gathered at the Communion Table, they have remembered as the Hebrews remembered the Exodus and in the same way have known the re-presentation of his death and his resurrection. All this happens again and again in our present— Christ is our Passover. We affirm with Paul as he writes to the Church at Corinth: 'For Christ our paschal lamb has been sacrificed' (I Cor. 5.7; see also John 1.29; Rev. 5.6, 8, 12, 13). And with the hymn-writer we too would sing:

> Low in adoration bending
> Now our hearts our God revere:
> Faith her aid to sight is lending:
> Though unseen the Lord is near:
> Ancient types and shadows ending,
> Christ our Paschal Lamb is here.

25 · **Sacrifices to the Lord** — *'olah, minchah, qorban, shelem, zebach, chatta'th, 'asham*

Throughout the Ancient Near East the practice of sacrifice is an essential part of the relationship between a man and his gods. The Hebrews were an integral part of this climate of thought and environment and shared in many of the ideas common to the age, without necessarily reproducing mechanically the beliefs of the surrounding peoples.

The motives behind the differing kinds of sacrifice are varied but the chief types of sacrifice may be classified as to whether they were thought of as being a gift or tribute, a means of effecting communion or of securing expiation for sin.

Sacrifice as gift and tribute.   Behind the idea of bringing a gift to the deity there may be varied motives. The sacrifice may be offered as a token of gratitude for crops and herds or the product of one's labour, thereby recognizing that all has come from God. This may be seen in the offering of first-fruits of herd and field (Deut. 26.1-3, 10-11; Ex. 13.2, 13; 22.29). Other motives may well have been earlier, the idea, for example, of providing sustenance for God, although this would be replaced by more refined concepts as the idea of God grew. So the psalmist rejects indignantly this view of God: 'Do I eat the flesh of bulls, or drink the blood of goats?' (Ps. 50.9-13). Again gifts may be offered in order to gain the future beneficence of God.

Three words are used to describe sacrifices which express the gift aspect of sacrifice. The first is *'olah* which is translated as 'burnt offering' and has a root meaning of 'to go up'. So in Lev. 1.9 we read: 'And the priest shall burn the whole on the altar, as a burnt offering, an offering by fire, a pleasing odour to the Lord' (see also vv. 10-13). A second term is *minchah*. This word is used in a straight-forward way for a gift in such a passage as Gen. 32.13 where Jacob meets Essau after his years of estrangement. 'So he lodged there that night and took from what he had with him a *minchah* for his brother Esau' (see also I Sam. 10.27;

Judg. 3.15). Later the term *minchah* is used of the cereal offering (see Lev. 2.1, 2, 8, 14, 15). The third term that contains the idea of gift is *qorban* which has a basic meaning of 'to approach', and so 'bring near'. In Num. 31.50 we read: 'And we have brought the *qorban* of the Lord what each man found . . . to make atonement for ourselves before the Lord.' The word translated 'brought' is a verbal form of the same root from which *qorban* comes. Literally it would read 'we have brought near the thing brought near,' that is, the offering or gift. See the New Testament echo of this in Mark 7.11: 'What you would have gained from me is Corban (that is, given to God).'

Sacrifice as communion. A second classification of sacrifice is that which emphasizes the element of communion, an establishing of fellowship between God and man. Such an offering is the peace-offering *shelem*. The central idea is that of wholeness, of being intact and probably the *shelem* is offered to restore such a fellowship between God and his worshippers, a relationship impaired by sin. The ritual connected with the *shelem* is found in Leviticus ch. 3 and differs from that of the burnt offering in that only portions of the animal are burnt on the altar and the rest is eaten by the worshippers (see Lev. 3.1-6). The climax of the *zebach shelamim* (sacrifice of peace offering) is the sacrificial meal. The phrase used in Lev. 3.1 *zebach shelamim* is really a combination of the old term *zebach* meaning slaughter and a form of *shelem*—peace offering. We find the sacrificial meal referred to in such passages as Ex. 32.6: 'And they rose up early on the morrow, and offered burnt offerings and brought peace offerings; and the people sat down to eat and drink, and rose up to play.' (See also Ex. 18.12; Deut. 12.7, 18; 14.23, 26; 15.20 with the recurring emphasis on eating and drinking 'before the Lord'.) At the sacred meal God is the honoured guest, hence the need to associate the *shelem* (peace offering) with rejoicing: 'They beheld God, and ate and drank' (Ex. 24.11). Thus God through the sacred meal confirmed the covenant with his people.

Sacrifice as expiation. In the Old Testament two kinds of sacrifices are directly linked with an expressed purpose, that is, to expiate sins. These are *chatta'th* and *'asham*—sin offerings and guilt offerings. The sin offering is used of sins committed unwittingly and primarily of a ritual kind (Lev. 5.1-3) especially through the violation of some prohibition (Lev. 4.2, 13, 22 and 27). Yet beyond the laws laid down in Leviticus chs. 4 and 5 we find that the sin offering is used at the consecration of a priest (Ex. 29.14), the annual purification of the altar (Lev. 16.16) and the purification of the people (Num. 6.10 f.). Guilt offerings are used of purification of lepers, sexual sins and purification of an unclean Nazirite (Lev. 14.10-20; 19.20-22; Num. 6.12). The main purpose of these sacrifices is that the effects of sin be removed. The instrument or organ by means of which this can be effected is the giving of life. Since life is in the blood (see Study 23), 'Therefore the blood of the sacrificial animal is exactly what is required to bring about atonement, i.e. the removal of sin and guilt.' Yet sacrifice is never thought of as a mechanical guarantee of the restoration of the relationship between God and man. The ritual of the Day of Atonement contained as an essential the confession of sins (Lev. 16.21) and the attitude of the offerer is of primary importance. Sacrifice is not something that man can do but that which God provides as an institution and rightly used he then accepts. 'And when they completed these days then from the eighth day onward the priest shall offer upon the altar your burnt offering and your peace offerings and I will accept you, says the Lord God' (Ezek. 43.27; 20.40f.)

Sacrifice is an instrument of grace more than a human device.

26 · The Law — *torah*

The hopes and dreams of the devout Hebrew are all crystallized in one word—the *Torah*—the Law. Even in the New Testament Jesus puts the matter in true perspective when he says, 'Think not that I have come to abolish the law and the prophets; I have come not to abolish them but to fulfil them' (Matt. 5.17). Behind the reverence for the Law there is a story part of which we may tell as we look at the various uses and contexts in which *torah* is found.

The pointer.   The scene in Exodus 15 where the Israelites seeking water in their journeyings come to Marah illustrates a use of the root from which *torah* comes. Because of the bitterness they cannot drink the water and protest: 'And the people murmured against Moses, saying, "What shall we drink?" And he cried to the Lord; and the Lord showed him a tree, and he threw it into the water' (vv. 24-25). The original for 'showed' means pointed out and uses the same verb *yarah* from which *torah* is derived. So also in Prov. 6.12-13 the worthless person is described: 'A worthless person, a wicked man, goes about with crooked speech, winks with his eyes, scrapes with his feet, points with his finger, with perverted heart devises evil, continually sowing discord.' The word for 'points' is again the same root *yarah*. In I Sam. 20.36 the same verb is used of shooting an arrow by Jonathan's servant lad. The central idea in the verb from which *torah* comes is that of pointing out or shooting in a certain direction.

The directive.   We find that *toroth*, the plural of *torah* is used of a series of directions as to conduct and behaviour. These may be called divine directives given by the priest in answer to those who have come to enquire of the Lord. So Moses speaks in Ex. 18.16, 'When they have a dispute, they come to me and I decide betweeen a man and his neighbour, and I make them know the statutes of God and his decisions.' The original for 'decisions' is *toroth*—the directives of God. Over a period of time a number of previous decisions would accummulate and a body or case-book of divine precedents would be formed. Thus in Hosea, the prophet attacks the leaders of the nation, priests and prophets in these words: 'My people are destroyed for lack of knowledge; because you have rejected knowledge, I reject you from being a priest to me. And since you have forgotten the law of your God I will also forget your children' (Hos. 4.6). The series of directives and decisions—the *toroth*—have become the *Torah*—the law of God.

The Law and the Way.   A striking feature of the use of *Torah* is its close association with the idea of the Way (*derek*). These two terms (*torah* and *derek*) are frequently found together. The idea of a direction has become wedded to the actual way that is taken. This is seen in Psalm 1: 'Blessed is the man who walks not in the counsel of the wicked, nor stands in the way of sinners, nor sits in the seat of scoffers; but his delight is in the law (*torah*) of the Lord, and on his (*torah*) law he meditates day and night . . . for the Lord knows the way of the righteous, but the way of the wicked will perish' (vv. 1-2, 6). And again in Psalm 25: 'All the paths of the Lord are steadfast love and faithfulness, for those who keep his covenant and his testimonies' (v. 10). The prophet Isaiah sounds the same note in saying, 'Come let us go up to the mountain of the Lord, to the house of the God of Jacob; that he may teach us his ways and that we may walk in his paths. For out of Zion shall go forth the law (*torah*) and the word of the Lord from Jerusalem' (Isa. 2.3). The word *torah* from being a pointer in a direction has become a way of life that is embodied in the Torah. The signpost has become the highway and even the destination, since the Law means more than the record of God's decisions. It develops to mean the revelation of God to his people at the deepest level.

The *Torah* must be seen as more than an external regulation of law laid down for successive generations. A recent comment has been, 'that fundamentally *torah* in the Old Testament denotes God's revelational decision and points to the guidance that God would give His people in their everyday life. . . . A translation of *torah* by "word of revelation" would come closer to the original meaning' (T. C. Vriezen, *An Outline of Old Testament Theology*, p. 256).

The Lord is the Way. The climax of the concept of the Way is found in John where Jesus replies to Thomas, 'I am the way, and the truth, and the life' (14.6). Christ is the fulfilment of God's revelation and he fulfils the Torah. The Law and the Way become One. As for ourselves, we too are of those who have been called the People of the Way (Acts 9.2). God offers to all people his *Torah* (Law) that is more than regulation. It is his self-revelation through Christ who is the Way. We must follow the direction of the Way with Christ, the companion of every step and goal at journey's end.

> Run the straight race through God's good grace,
> Lift up thine eyes, and seek His face;
> Life with its way before us lies;
> Christ is the path, and Christ the prize.

27 · **The Remnant** — *shear-jashub*

What shall we call him? One of the most intimate occasions in family life is the day when a name is chosen for a child. How the prophet Isaiah answered this age-long question in a striking way is described in Isa. 7.3: 'And the Lord said to Isaiah, go forth to meet Ahaz, you and Shear-Jashub, your son, at the end of the conduit of the upper pool on the highway to the Fuller's Field. . . .' *Shear-jashub*, that is, 'a remnant shall return'. What a name to give a child! Yet this name embodies one of the greatest affirmations and convictions of the Old Testament, even of the whole Bible.

Anticipations of the remnant in early history. We are prepared for this concept of remnant as it emerges in the unfolding story of God's dealing with his people. The first glimpse is found in the encounter between God and Noah. Mankind has proved itself evil but God does not destroy all mankind. His dilemma is pictured in Gen. 6.5: 'The Lord saw that the wickedness of man was great in the earth, and that every imagination of the thoughts of his heart was only evil continually. And the Lord was sorry that he has made man on the earth and it grieved him to his heart. So the Lord said, "I will blot out man whom I have created from the face of the earth. . . ." But Noah found favour in the eyes of the Lord.' So in Noah and his family we have an early 'remnant' saved by God to continue his purpose. Again in the story of Joseph we have the account of his poignant revelation of his identity to his own brothers who thought him dead, and at their hands. This was their own doing so they thought, but the truer story is described by Joseph: 'And do not be distressed or angry with yourselves, because you sold me here; for God sent me before you to preserve life' (Gen. 45.5); 'And God sent me before you to preserve for you a remnant on earth, and to keep alive for you many survivors. So it was not you who sent me here, but God' (vv. 7-8).

A further anticipation of the remnant concept is found in the answer that God gave to Elijah at Horeb when he passionately protests that he is no better than his fathers so he had better die. The reply is salutary to the prophet in his despairing mood: 'Yet I will leave seven thousand in Israel, all the knees that have not bowed to Baal, and every mouth that has not kissed him' (I Kings 19.18).

The remnant that means judgment.   One of the basic ideas behind the remnant concept is certainly that of judgment. The Israelites have rebelled and refused to amend their ways. The prophet sees all too clearly that judgment is certain: 'In that day the remnant of Israel and the survivors of the house of Jacob will no more lean upon him that smote them, but will lean upon the Lord, the Holy One of Israel, in truth. A remnant will return, the remnant of Jacob, to the mighty God. For though your people Israel be as the sand of the sea, only a remnant of them will return. Destruction is decreed, overflowing with righteousness' (Isa. 10.20-22). The same note is heard in the prophecy of Zephaniah: 'For then I will remove from your midst your proudly exultant ones, and you shall no longer be haughty in my holy mountain. For I will leave in the midst of you a people humble and lowly. They shall seek refuge in the name of the Lord ...' (Zeph. 3.11-12).

The remnant that means hope.   Yet judgment does not exhaust all that the prophets meant by *shear*—remnant. It is used in passages that are charged with a new positive meaning of hope. Whatever disaster befalls, at least a remnant will be saved to be the instrument of God's purpose in a new age. This note is heard in such passages as: 'And though a tenth remain in it, it will be burned again like a terebinth or an oak whose stump remains standing when it is felled. The holy seed is its stump' (Isa. 6.13). And further in Jeremiah we find the prophet charged with the commission of pronouncing judgment by means of exile, yet still bearing witness: 'Then will I gather the remnant of my flock out of all the countries where I have driven them, and I will bring them back to the fold ... and they shall fear no more, nor be dismayed, neither shall any be missing, says the Lord' (Jer. 23.3-4).

The remnant as the nucleus of the Church.   As the Bible story unfolds we see a relationship between the remnant and the Church that is to be. In Isaiah such a link is present in the prophet's mind when he writes: 'Behold, I am laying in Zion for a foundation, a stone, a tested stone, a precious cornerstone, of a sure foundation' (Isa. 28.16). The actual word remnant is not used but the idea is central.

So we find the remnant theme continued in the New Testament and especially in Mark 14: 'And he came the third time and said to them, "Are you still sleeping and taking your rest? It is enough; the hour has come; the Son of Man is betrayed into the hands of sinners"' (Mark 14.41). Jesus in his own person has become the *Remnant of One*. From this remnant figure who becomes the Risen Lord the whole living Church grows and becomes the hope of the world.

28 · **Positive Peace** — *shalom*

Peace we all feel must mean something more than the absence of war. Our hope and instinctive feeling are right in line with the Old Testament word—*shalom*—which usually translated 'peace' has a far wider range of meaning.

We find *shalom* used in a number of contexts all of which have the idea of wholeness, of being intact or complete. For example, in Neh. 6.15 it is used of completing the building of a wall and in Isa. 60.20 of completing a period of time. Further, in the Book of Job we read: 'He is wise in heart and mighty in strength—who has hardened himself against him, and succeeded?' (Job 9.4). The context refers to a man contending with God and the original for 'and succeeded' means 'has kept himself whole, intact', using the same root from which *shalom* comes. A last example is found in the Psalter. In Ps. 65.1 we read: 'Praise is due to thee, O God, in Zion; and to thee shall vows be performed.' The root of the word translated 'performed' is the same as *shalom*. To repay that which is vowed or promised is to make whole again by repaying or restoring.

With the pointers given in the examples quoted we shall be able to trace the various strands in the pattern of relationships that we call peace.

Peace includes all that we mean by welfare.   In Isa. 32.16-18 we have a picture of a new society: 'Then justice will dwell in the wilderness, and righteousness abide in the fruitful field. And the effect of righteousness will be peace, and the result of righteousness, quietness and trust for ever. My people will abide in a peaceful habitation, in secure dwellings, and in quiet resting places.' This reads like a description of what we call a Welfare Society. This is certainly what *shalom* does mean. The role of moral conscience and passionate concern that we link with modern concepts of welfare are found in the prophetic emphasis on righteousness that results in peace. In a world of apartheid and under-privileged people we see that the Old Testament is right in affirming that *shalom* (peace) presupposes justice and then welfare.

Peace means the victory of God's purpose.   The second feature of *shalom* is its association with the proclamation of the new age. Let us look at such an ideal picture. 'For to us a child is born, to us a son is given: and the government will be upon his shoulder and his name will be called "Wonderful Counsellor, Mighty God, Everlasting Father, Prince of Peace". Of the increase of his government and of peace there will be no end' (Isa. 9.6-7). This is much more profound than any idea of a good time coming, be it ever so far away. The new age when God's purpose must be finally worked out will be a time of peace without end. We feel the dynamic, positive nature of peace. It means the victory of God's purpose and cannot be reached in a society that rejects his will. Peace expresses and demands the ultimate victory of God.

Peace given by God not gained by men.   Although on the human side peace is the outcome of justice and righteousness in social relationships, the ultimate source is God. We see this illustrated when we follow the idea of peace into the New Testament where the equivalent of *shalom* is *eirene*. In two passages the divine initiative is underlined. The familiar verse in the Beatitudes, 'Blessed are the peace-makers, for they shall be called sons of God' (Matt. 5.9) suggests this. In the thought of the Bible to be called 'sons of' means to share in the same nature—in this case, as God. Peacemaking is the outcome of being like God. Again, in the last days of his life on earth Jesus told his disciples of his legacy to them, 'Peace I leave with you; my peace I give unto you' (John 14.27). Peace is given, not engineered. So Paul in his letter to the Galatians writes of the fruits of the Spirit and in his list includes peace (Gal. 5.22).

Peace as personal relationship with Christ.   The climax of the biblical teaching concerning peace is reached in the affirmation that Paul makes in another of his letters, written to the church at Ephesus: 'For he is our peace, who has made us both one, and has broken down the dividing wall of hostility' (Eph. 2.14). He is our peace because he brings together in one whole all parts of the human family. He completes, makes intact again, the whole of mankind. This is indeed the heart of *shalom*, our starting-point. Welfare, the victory of God's purpose, the acceptance of a God-given peace and the challenge of a personal relationship with Christ are all the things that belong to our peace (Luke 19.42).

29 · Covenant — *berith*

One of the greatest concepts of the Bible is contained in the very name that we give to its two divisions—the Old and New Testaments. The word translated 'testament' means 'covenant' and the Bible is the story of God's covenant relationship with men. We are the people of the covenant and the Bible is the Book of the Covenant—Old and New.

The word translated 'covenant' in the Old Testament is *berith* and throughout the Bible story we see emphasis laid upon it.

Unfolding Covenant. A brief survey will bring out the dominance of the concept of *berith*—covenant. At the very birth of the Hebrew people God makes a covenant with Abraham (Gen. 17.2) and even in the early stories of Genesis before the patriarchs we see that God affirms the covenant relationship with Noah after the experience of the Flood, as he gives mankind another chance. So through the Bible story at all the great pivotal moments God affirms the covenant. The giving of the Decalogue is within a covenant setting (Ex. 19.5-20.17) and the spiritual pilgrimage of Jeremiah reaches its climax in the concept of the Inner Covenant (Jer. 31.31-34). The agony of the Exile as described by Second Isaiah is also seen and interpreted through the idea of the continuing covenant. God tells the prophet that it is too small and light a task for the Hebrew people to undergo the travail and

suffering of the Exile just to return and keep themselves to themselves in a cocoon of narrow nationalism. They must become a
covenant to the rest of the world (Isa. 42.6; see also Isa. 49.8).

The New Covenant.   Right on into the book of the New Covenant, which is exactly the meaning of the New Testament, we may
trace this key motif. Two scenes spring readily to mind. The first
is the Upper Room. During the last meal of fellowship with his
disciples Jesus reinforces the words of Jeremiah concerning the
Inner Covenant when he says, 'This is my body' and 'This is the
New covenant in my blood' (Mark. 14.22-24; I Cor. 11.23-26).
We come, further, to the closing scenes of the Bible where the
New Jerusalem is pictured by the Seer of Patmos. The new
heaven and earth are portrayed and a voice is heard: 'Behold,
the tabernacle of God is with men, and he shall dwell with them
and they shall be his people, and God himself shall be with them
and be their God' (Rev. 21.3 and Jer. 31.33). Clearly, the story
of the Bible is the Story of the Covenant.

In the following contexts we may underline the main characteristics of the use of *berith*—covenant.

The Covenant is always initiated by God.   The Covenant is
described as the gift of God to man rather than any relationship
that is earned or deserved because the Hebrews were better than
other people (Gen. 9.17; 17.7). We are reminded of the words of
Jesus in John 15.16, 'You did not choose me but I chose you and
appointed you.' We are covenant people in response to his initiation. He calls and we respond and this makes us responsible
people.

The Covenant as a relationship between unequals.   The idea that
God and the Hebrews came together as if to sign any contract,
offering mutual benefit, is completely alien to the thought of the
Bible. In the latest Hebrew lexicon we are told that *berith* is used
of the table-fellowship that a strong man offers to a sick, weak
man. The strong-weak relationship with all its problems are
crystallized here. The strong must covenant their strength on be-

half of the weak in every sphere. The covenant is not a contract and no man may give God notice that he is contracting out of any obligation to him. (See Josh. 9.3-15; I Sam. 11.1ff.; I Kings 20.34; Gen. 26.28).

The Covenant involves the community. There are but few references in the Old Testament to God making a covenant with individuals (see II Sam. 23.5; Ps. 89.4, 29). Even in such cases the individual must be seen within the context of the community. There can be no private treaties with God. God does speak in personal encounter but the result of such meeting must involve the community (see Jer. 32.36-40). There is no support in the covenant idea for the solitary Christian.

The Covenant engages the whole personality. One of the striking features of the deepening experience of the Hebrews is the development and transition from the written law of the Decalogue to the inner covenant of Jeremiah—'But this is the covenant which I will make with the house of Israel after these days, says the Lord: I will put my law within them, and I will write it upon their hearts; and I will be their God, and they shall be my people' (Jer. 31.33). The old covenant reaches its fulfilment in the commitment of the total personality rather than obedience to a set of external rules. The Covenant becomes personal when Jesus, proceeding from the thought of Jeremiah, affirms: 'This cup is the new covenant in my blood' (I Cor. 11.25).

The Covenant demands mission. The very purpose of God's initiation of his covenant with the Hebrews is that all men might enter the same relationship. The inner urge to mission is integral from the outset in the call to Abraham (Gen. 17.3). Of particular relevance are the words of Deutero-Isaiah after the Exile when he faces the danger of the Hebrews turning inwards upon themselves. They must listen to the word of God: 'I have kept you and given you as a covenant to the people' (Isa. 49.8). Covenant involves mission by its very nature.

30 · The Satan — *ha-satan*

The title of this study may seem a bit strange. Why *the* Satan? Why not just Satan or even satan with a small s? A glance at a few passages containing this Hebrew word *satan* will help us to understand. In I Sam. 29.4 we read of the encounter between David and Achish. The commanders of the Philistines refuse to allow David to fight with them in case he should prove a defaulter although he has been an outlaw in the service of the king of Gath for some time. The verse runs, 'But the commanders of the Philistines were angry with him; and the commanders of the Philistines said to him; "Send the man back, that he may return to the place which you have assigned him; he shall not go down with us to battle, lest he become an adversary to us. For how could this fellow reconcile himself to his lord? would it not be with the heads of the men here?"' The word translated 'adversary' is the Hebrew *satan* and the basic meaning is one who opposes the will and purpose of another. There is no suggestion here of any theological content as a rival to God. A further passage illustrates the use of *satan* in the story of Balaam. In Numbers 22 we read: 'So Balaam rose in the morning and saddled his ass, and went with the princes of Moab. But God's anger was kindled because he went; and the angel of the Lord took his stand in the way as his adversary (*satan*)' (vv. 21-22). Later in the same chapter we read (v. 32): 'And the angel of the Lord said to him, "Why have you struck your ass three times? Behold, I have come forth to withstand you, because your way is perverse before me."' The original for 'withstand' is 'to act the part of a satan', that is, an opponent, one who crosses one's purpose. Again in Psalm 71 we have, 'O God, be not far from me; O my God, make haste to help me! May my accusers be put to shame and consumed; with scorn and disgrace may they be covered who seek my hurt.' The literal meaning of 'my accusers' is 'my satans'. Similarly, in Ps. 109.6 we read: 'Appoint a wicked man against him; let an accuser bring him to trial.' Behind all these passages, the use of the word *satan* is to represent a function, that of putting one-self against another. There is no reference to the person involved and certainly the word has no meaning as a personal name with the capital S.

The Satan in the Book of Job. When we come to the Prologue of Job the entry of *the Satan* upon the scene is described in these words: 'Now there was a day when the sons of God came to present themselves before the Lord, and (the) Satan also came among them. The Lord said to (the) Satan, "Whence have you come?" (The) Satan answered the Lord, "From going to and fro on the earth, and from walking up and down in it." ' As the rest of the Prologue unfolds we see that the function of the Satan (the Hebrew has the article in each instance) is to probe and sift the integrity of those who say that they love the Lord, in case there are any strings attached! The Satan is like some undercover agent whose job it is to report on the loyalty of a king's subjects. By the nature of his work and the sort of report he would frequently make, he would become regarded as an informer and so an adversary and opponent. The Satan doubts whether God is such that a man will serve him without some reward or return. He turns to God who himself has drawn attention to Job as a blameless upright man, and insinuates, 'Does Job fear God for nought?' (Job 1.6-7, 9). There is no question at this stage of the Satan being opposed to God. He is among the children of God and carries out a function on God's behalf. He is a Prosecutor General but God is still fundamentally alone in charge of his world. The Satan is as yet the servant of God and the adversary only of men and then on God's behalf. (See Zech. 3.1-5.)

Satan as Anti-God. The concept of the Satan does not remain static and largely due to the influence of Persian religion we reach in the Old Testament the usage of the word *Satan* to represent the Evil One who although inferior and subordinate opposes God as long as this world lasts. So in the late passage I Chron. 21.1 we read: 'And Satan stood up against Israel and provoked David to number Israel.' In this passage the article does not occur with Satan. It is striking to note that the earlier version of this incident in II Sam. 24.1 states that God himself is responsible for driving David to this act of folly. In the rest of the Bible it is clear that the concept of Satan has changed in two vital respects. (See Matt. 25.41; Rev. 2.13; 12.7, 9.) The name for a function has changed to the name of a personal being and the satan has become Satan and from being one of the servants of God he has become a rival power. So in the apocryphal book of Wisdom we read: 'but through the devil's envy death entered the world, and those who belong to his party experience it' (Wisdom 2.24).

As a result of our examination of the way that the word *satan* is used we reaffirm that the dualism of a conflicting God and Satan is alien to the Old Testament. We may make our own the verdict of Vriezen in his *Outline of Old Testament Theology* when he comments, 'The doctrine of Satan is due to a more profound spiritual understanding of God, who is too holy to countenance sin. In Israel God's Being becomes more and more ethical and transcendental, so that Evil can no longer be regarded as coming from Him, but is detached from God in the figure of Satan' (p. 156).

The final answer to the concept of Satan as it developed is found in such an affirmation as that of Paul: 'For I am sure that neither death, nor life, nor angels, nor principalities, nor things present, nor things to come, nor powers, nor height, nor depth, nor anything else in creation, will be able to separate us from the love of God in Christ Jesus our Lord' (Rom. 8.38-39).

31 · The Anointed One — *mashiach*

Since the glorious music of Handel has become wedded to the poignant words of the prophet Isaiah there can hardly be a single person who doesn't know at least this word *mashiach* in the more familiar form of *messiah*. At the Festival of the Birth of Christ and again at the triumphal celebration of Easter, men and women are helped through the medium of oratorio as words of scripture winged by haunting music are made to live as they consider anew the one who was despised and rejected of men, the *Messiah*. In this brief study we shall trace the different ways in which the word *mashiach* or *messiah* is used in the Bible. In Ex. 29.2 which describes the consecration of the sons of Aaron we read: 'Now this is what you shall do to them, that they may serve me as priests. Take one young bull and two rams without blemish, and unleavened bread, unleavened cakes mixed with oil, and unleavened wafers spread with oil.' The phrase 'spread with oil' is a translation of the original root—*mashach*—to spread. It is from this root that the word *mashiach* comes. Again in Isa. 21.5, a prophetic oracle concerning Babylon, we read: 'My mind reels, horror has appalled me; the twilight I longed for has been turned for me into trembling. They prepare the table, they spread the rugs, they eat, they drink. Arise, O princes, oil the shield!' The imperative —oil the shield—refers to the practice of oiling the shield to keep it smooth so that the arrows of the enemy might ricochet from it. (See II Sam. 1.21.) The literal meaning 'spread with oil' might also be translated 'anoint the shield'.

The anointed one as king.   The main usage of anointing is seen in the setting apart of a person to a special office. Once anointed such a person is a *mashiach*, an anointed one. It is of particular significance when used of the coronation of a king. In I Sam. 15.1 and 17, Samuel addresses Saul: 'And Samuel said to Saul, "The Lord sent me to anoint you king over his people Israel." And Samuel said, "Though you are little in your own eyes, are you not the head of the tribes of Israel? The Lord anointed you king over Israel." '

The Messiah as priest.   The term is also applied to the priests, as for example, Aaron's sons. 'And for Aaron's sons you shall make coat and girdles and caps; you shall make them for glory and beauty. And you shall put them upon Aaron, your brother and upon his sons with him, and you shall anoint them and ordain

them and consecrate them, that they may serve me as priests'
(Ex. 28.40-41).

The Messiah as prophet.   The prophet too may be a *mashiach*
since he is an anointed one. So in I Kings 19.15 God tells Elijah
after his fit of depression in the cave at Horeb: 'Go, return on your
way to the wilderness of Damascus; and when you arrive, you
shall anoint Hazael to be king over Israel; and Elisha, the son of
Abel-meholah you shall anoint to be prophet in your place.'

The Messiah as patriarch.   In Psalm 105 we find the term applied to the patriarchs Abraham, Isaac and Jacob. The psalmist
pictures God speaking to the kings of the earth: 'Touch not my
anointed ones, do my prophets no harm!' (v. 15). The parallelism
with 'my prophets' indicates that the writer regarded the patriarchs as the recipients and custodians of divine revelation
as were the prophets of a later day (see Gen. 20.7 where the term
'prophet' is applied to Abraham).

The Messiah belonging to another nation.   One of the greatest
insights into the meaning of *mashiach* is the way that it is used
in Isa. 45.1 where God speaks and applies the term to a member
of another race: 'Thus says the Lord to his anointed, to Cyrus,
whose right hand I have grasped, to subdue nations before him
and ungird the loins of kings, to open doors before him that gates
may not be closed ... I gird you, though you do not know me'
(vv. 1 and 5). As there is but One God so the Anointed One, the
Messiah belongs to the world and is not the exclusive possession
of one nation.

The Messiah and the Suffering Servant.   The climax of the use
of *mashiach* is reached when the transition is made from the con-
quering messiah in fields of economic and political power to the
suffering Messiah who founds a church not an empire. Jesus himself offers this interpretation of his own mission: 'For the Son of
Man also came not to be served but to serve, and to give his life a
ransom for many' (see Mark 10.45 and Isa. 53.5, 12). Jesus in

his public manifesto goes back to Isa. 61.1-2 for the very terms of his programme: 'The Spirit of the Lord is upon me, because he has anointed me to preach good news to the poor. He has sent me to proclaim release to the captives, and recovery of sight to the blind, to set at liberty those who are oppressed, to proclaim the acceptable year of the Lord' (Luke 4.18-19). We must note, 'he has anointed me', that is, this is my mission: to merge the role of Suffering Servant with that of the Messiah and the Son of Man. A comment by Koehler has been, 'At this point the theology of the Old Testament comes to an end' (*Old Testament Theology,* p. 238). This may very well be, and we may add, the theology of the New Testament begins. When Peter replies to the question of Jesus, Who do you say that I am? You are the Christ, the Son of the Living God, he is saying that Jesus is the Anointed One—the Messiah. (See Matt. 16.16.) The very word 'Christ' is but saying 'Anointed one' or Messiah in another language. The Messiah is supremely the Christ, Son of the Living God.

32 · The Redeemer — *go'el*

And didst Thou love the race that loved not Thee?
And didst Thou take to heaven a human brow?
Dost plead with man's voice by the marvellous sea?
Art Thou his kinsman now?

These moving words of Jean Ingelow contain a word that we more readily recognize as the familiar 'redeemer'. It is the word 'kinsman'. The relation between 'redeemer' and 'kinsman' is seen when we examine the use of the Hebrew *go'el* which comes from *ga'al* meaning to protect and then redeem. It is found in such a passage as the cry of Job:

Oh that my words were written!
Oh that they were inscribed in a book!
Oh that with an iron pen and lead they were graven in the rock
for ever!

For I know that my Redeemer lives, and that at the last he will
stand upon the earth (Job 19.23-25).

Two scenes will illustrate the meaning of the word. In Josh.
20.2-3 the Cities of Refuge are set apart to provide sanctuary for
those who are guilty of manslaughter through some accident,
without intention. Here such persons could flee from the one who
is nearest of kin to the dead person. This man is the 'avenger of
blood' and the word *go'el* is used for 'avenger'. It is his duty to
avenge blood that has been shed (see Deut. 19.6; II Sam. 14.11).
A second scene underlines a further right and duty of the kinsman,
that is, to marry the widow of a nearest relation in order to continue his name, and in Hebrew thought, his personality. So we
read that Boaz says to Ruth in answer to her plea that he act as
her kinsman, that is, her redeemer: 'And now it is true that I am a
near kinsman yet there is a kinsman nearer than I . . . but if he is
not willing to do the part of the next of kin for you, then as the
Lord lives, I will do the part of the next of kin for you' (Ruth
3.12-13). The next of kin is the *go'el*. A number of characteristics
of the use of *go'el* (redeemer) may be noted.

Redemption presupposes relationship before rules. One of the
striking facts about the Bible story is that the very foundation
of belief in God is the certainty that God has acted to redeem his
people. The most important part of the Ten Commandments is in
the preamble: 'I am the Lord your God who has brought you
out of the land of Egypt, out of the house of bondage' (Ex. 20.2).
Then follow the rules for living consequent upon the redemption.
Similarly, the Psalmist speaks, 'Remember thy congregation,
which thou hast gotten of old, which thou hast redeemed to be
the tribe of thy heritage' (Ps. 74.2). The first passage does not use
the word *go'el*, but the idea of redemption as of a slave (Lev.
25.42, 48-9) is clearly present and a form of the same root from
which *go'el* comes is used by the psalmist. It is because the
Hebrews were redeemed by God that they realized they were his
own people and so they must live in accordance with his word.

They were to be good because they were God's people. They were not God's people because they were good. Redemption then the Rules.

Redemption is spiritual as well as material. The idea of redeeming a people or an individual is always linked with a situation of crisis. Blood has been shed, a husband has died, a person is in slavery or a nation in exile—each situation demands a *go'el*, a near kinsman or redeemer. The word is used with a meaning beyond that of merely material restoration. It comes to be used of spiritual reconciling. We see this in Psalm 103: 'Bless the Lord, O my soul, and forget not all his benefits, who forgives all your iniquity, who heals all your disease, who redeems your life from the Pit, who crowns you with steadfast love and mercy . . .' (vv. 2-4; see also Isa. 52.9). Redemption involves more than an escape from a dangerous physical plight. It means a renewal of a spiritual relationship.

Redemption as a family decision. Again and again in the Old Testament it is underlined that the *go'el* is the near kinsman, a member of the family. The redeemer and the redeemed belong. In a profound sense, this is true of God's dealings with men, as Job felt he belonged to his Redeemer who would stand by him and vindicate him (Job. 19.23-25 quoted above). God in his redeeming of Israel from Egypt and the Exile is acting within the family context. Supremely at the Cross on Calvary we know we are members of the family of God. Made in his image we are of the same kin and in the crisis of sin we desperately need our near Kinsman, our Redeemer, our *Go'el*. This is the heart of the affirmation of Easter that in Christ we have our Redeemer, our *Go'el* and we know he lives!

It is precisely because Christ is our Kinsman and redeems us that we must share this knowledge with all who are our kind, our kin, that is all human-kind. We are committed by the very challenge of this word *go'el* to proclaim that we are bound together beyond divisions of race or colour.

By that one likeness which is ours and Thine,
By that one nature which doth hold us kin,
By that high heaven where, sinless Thou dost shine
To draw us sinners in.

33 · The Abode of the Dead — *She'ol*

Life for men and women living in Old Testament times had to be carried on against the one certainty that it held—it would all end in *She'ol*. Sheol was the dread final curtain to all the hopes and dreams, the longings and aspirations. This was the accepted belief yet we find recorded some slight tearing of the veil between this life and the next in a number of passages. We shall see what audacity is contained in such leaps of faith as we look briefly at what the Old Testament meant by its use of the word *She'ol* to describe the grave and abode of the dead.

This is the underworld where the dead descended after life on earth. A gigantic underground cavern where there is an existence of a kind for creatures that are called the Shades or shadowy ones. In the Old Testament we need again and again to remember that all human life is to be measured against this concept of dread that is described in some of the following ways.

The no-world. When a person dies he goes to the land of no-return and Job expresses this in poignant terms: 'The eye of him who sees me will behold me no more; while thy eyes are upon me, I shall be gone. As the cloud fades and vanishes so he who goes down to Sheol does not come up; he returns no more to his house, nor does his place know him any more' (Job 7.8-10). Not only does man not return but there in Sheol the ultimate tragedy is that there he may not praise God and God cannot reveal his covenant-love. There is no communion between God and man in this no-world. This we see in the outburst of the psalmist: 'Every day I call upon thee, O Lord; I spread my hands to thee. Dost thou work wonders for the dead? Do the shades rise up to praise thee? Is thy steadfast love declared in the grave, or thy faithfulness in Abaddon? Are thy wonders known in the darkness, or thy saving help in the land of forgetfulness?' (Ps. 88.9-12). The psalmist is pleading with God that he show forth his power now when he can because when Sheol comes even God the creator of the world can do nothing. This is the remorseless logic of Sheol. It is indeed the No-World. (See also Isa. 38.18; Job 26.5; Jonah 2.3.)

The break-through.   The presupposition of the passages we have looked at so far is that God has no power or authority, no terms of reference, that include *Sheol*. The Hebrew mind could not remain content with the living God shut out of Sheol. As the range of God's lordship was seen to grow and as the intimacy of communion with him increased there are voices heard that dare to question old beliefs. We find a break-through of the human spirit created in God's image. In a number of passages we find the older belief in Sheol disintegrating. So in the Song of Hannah we read: 'The Lord kills and brings to life; he brings down to Sheol and raises up' (I Sam. 2.6). In the prophet Amos we find: 'Though they dig into Sheol, from there shall my hand take them; though they climb up to heaven, from there will I bring them down' (Amos 9.2). It is a world of moral causation and even in Sheol God is now believed to have power. In a more positive way as a result of the experience of living in communion with God the psalmist rejoices in the wonder of God's abiding nearness: 'Whither shall I go from thy Spirit? Or whither shall I flee from thy presence? If I ascend to heaven, thou art there! If I make my bed in Sheol, thou art there!' (Ps. 139.7-8). It is significant that the Old Testament knows nothing of a Sheol as an after-world of torment and suffering where punishment is meted out. Later in the development of Hebrew thought and due largely to Persian influences we have the concepts of Gehenna with the apocalyptic characteristics of eternal punishment (Matt. 25.41; Rev. 20.14) but the original Sheol belief carries no such meaning.

Glimpses of communion. The very bankruptcy of Sheol leads to some glimpses of a worthwhile life after death with a continuing communion between God and man. Such we find if only tentatively in the Book of Job and the Psalter. The affirmation of Job contains this leap of faith: 'For I know that my Redeemer lives, and that at the last he will stand upon the earth; and after my skin has been thus destroyed, then without my flesh I shall see God' (Job 19.25-26). Job is convinced that Sheol is not the last word. The precise manner in which Job would see God the present text does not allow us to say, 'but its certain expectation is there. It shows like a beacon light over the tumult' (Terrien on Job in the *Interpreter's Bible*).

Of striking significance is the picture of God 'taking' or 'receiving' a man so that he is rescued from Sheol. Thus in the account of Enoch's life we read, 'Enoch walked with God; and he was not for God took him' (Gen. 5.24). The word translated 'took' is *laqach* and is found again in the story of Elijah: 'When they had crossed, Elijah said to Elisha, "Ask what I shall do for you, before I am taken from you" ' (II Kings 2.9). The psalmists use precisely the same word. In Psalm 49 the psalmist sees that evil men are appointed for Sheol but for himself he believes, 'But God will ransom my soul from the power of Sheol, for he will receive me' (vv. 14-15). In Psalm 73 the writer after wrestling with the problem of the prosperity of the wicked and the suffering of the righteous reaches this conviction: 'Nevertheless, I am continually with thee; thou dost hold my right hand. Thou dost guide me with thy counsel, and afterward thou wilt receive me to glory' (vv. 23-24). The way ahead is pointed out—communion with God is such that it must continue and the dread poverty of Sheol is revealed by the very intensity of the psalmist's affirmation. These glimpses are underlined by the experience of the persecutions and martyrdoms of the Maccabean period and belief in another life is strengthened (see Dan. 12.2). Here we find the first articulated rejection of the finality of Sheol.

These brief insights mark the beginning of the pilgrimage that reaches its climax in the Easter victory:

> Vain the stone, the watch, the seal;
>   Christ hath burst the gates of hell:
> Death in vain forbids His rise;
>   Christ hath opened Paradise.

FOR FURTHER READING

J. J. von Allmen (ed.), *Vocabulary of the Bible*, Lutterworth, 1956

B. W. Anderson, *The Living World of the Old Testament*, Longmans, Green, 1958

E. Jacob, *Theology of the Old Testament*, Hodder and Stoughton, 1958

L. Koehler, *Old Testament Theology*, Lutterworth, 1957

A. Richardson (ed.), *A Theological Word Book of the Bible*, SCM, 1950

H. H. Rowley, *The Faith of Israel*, SCM, 1956

N. H. Snaith, *The Distinctive Ideas of the Old Testament*, Epworth, 1944

T. C. Vriezen, *An Outline of Old Testament Theology*, Blackwell, 1958

MORE ADVANCED WORKS

James Barr, *The Semantics of Biblical Language*, O.U.P., 1961

W. Eichrodt, *Theology of the Old Testament*, vol. I, SCM, 1961

G. von Rad, *Old Testament Theology*, vol. I, Oliver and Boyd, 1962

INDEX OF HEBREW WORDS

INDEX OF SCRIPTURE REFERENCES
(Revised Standard Version)
OLD TESTAMENT